Forest Resource Management and Tribal Women (Abuá Bir)

About the Author

Dr. Prabhawati Bodra has done M.Sc (Botany) and Ph.D. from Ranchi University, Ranchi. At present, she is Assistant Professor at University Department of Botany, Sido Kanhu Murmu University, Dumka, Jharkhand. The University was founded in 1992 and named after two great Santhal martyrs Sido and Kanhu Murmu who led the "The Hul" against British Raj in 1855. The University stands as a milestone in this region for higher education and human development.

The author is an avid worker in the field of ethnobotany and engaged in research of tribals association with forest flora especially of Jharkhand. Many articles and a book have been published in this regard. At present, she is also engrossed in study of traditional herbal remediation practiced by Santhals and inventorying it under UGC sponsorship and other related works of ethnobotany.

Forest Resource Management and Tribal Women

(Abuá Bir)

Prabhawati Bodra

CONCEPT PUBLISHING COMPANY PVT. LTD.
NEW DELHI-110059

ISBN: 978-93-86682-89-5

First Published 2021

Published and Printed by

Concept
Since 1974

Concept Publishing Company Pvt. Ltd.
A/15-16, Commercial Block, Mohan Garden,
New Delhi-110059 (INDIA)
T: 91 11 41101460, 91 11 25351460, 91 11 25351794
E : publishing@conceptpub.com, *W*: www.conceptpub.com

Cataloging in Publication Data--Courtesy: D.K. Agencies (P) Ltd. <docinfo@dkagencies.com>

Bodra, Prabhawati, author.
Forest resource management and tribal women (Abuá Bir) / Prabhawati Bodra.
pages cm
Includes bibliographical references and index.
ISBN 9789386682895

1. Forest management--India--Jharkhand. 2. Traditional medicine--India--Jharkhand. 3. Tribes--India--Jharkhand--Social life and customs. 4. Rural women--India--Jharkhand. 5. Rural women--Health and hygiene--India--Jharkhand. I. Title.

LCC SD646.J43B63 2021 | DDC 634.920954127 23

I dedicate this book
to my parents
Late Theodore Bodra and Late Abinashi Bodra,
from whom I have inherited the virtue of compassion

Foreword

I have great pleasure in writing this Foreword of this small book "Forest Resource Management and Tribal Women—Abuá Bir" meaning "Our forest" written by Dr. Prabhawati Bodra, who is known to me since her childhood. Her father late Mr. Theodore Bodra was a Forest Minister of the then Undivided Bihar State, was well acquainted with me. Miss Prabhawati was a M.Sc. Botany student of the special paper "Physiology of Plant Growth and Development" in Ranchi University, which was started on my application and she also did her Ph.D. research under my supervision. She has a feeling for the plants and that feeling of a lady who was born and brought up amidst dense forest of the spent years of childhood and youth is being reflected in this attempt of her in the intense inner feelings and sentlments complied with scientific knowledge of the importance of plants of the forests.

I hope, the persons having an interest in environment and welfare of mankind would enjoy going through this book, which reflects the intense human feelings about this contribution of forest in our lives of past, present and future!

Dr. K.K. Nag

Former Professor and Head,
Department of Botany,
Ranchi University
Former Vice Chancellor
(Bhagalpur, Ranchi & Vinoba Bhave University)
Rameshwaram, Bariatu Road, Ranchi-834009
Jharkhand

02.3.2018

Preface

Since childhood, I have always been in contact with villagers residing in the close proximity of forest and have shared many exquisite moments, which are now part of my fond memories. With the passing time, I got more influenced with their life pattern owing to increase in familiarity with tribal people. The interrelationship of a tribal woman with nature is wondrous. It is a beautiful blending of life and nature. It inspired me to reflect her life in words.

The title of the book is "Forest Resource Management and Tribal Women—Abuá Bir" is a Mundari word (one of the tribal languages of Jharkhand) meaning "our forest". The social pattern of the tribals is based on community solidarity. Stress is always laid on the group instead of an individual. "Our" is always more precise than "my", but in this treatise the emphasis is laid to the relationship of an individual woman and her connection with the natural forest. She represents other females of her society and based on her perspective the concept is developed. I honestly feel she represents not only her community, but embodies all women globally whose life support system is the natural biota. From the window of a tribal woman's life, the book presents a short view of the intersection of the aesthetic and economic lives of the tribal community. It tries to highlight the harmony with which the natural and cultural habitats of the community supplement and nourish each other.

In this book, I have tried to draw a somewhat cross-disciplinary portrait of a tribal woman's life-long dependency on the natural flora through expression of her relentless labour, ethno-botanical knowledge, economic status, and socio-cultural behaviour in relation to the forest biodiversity. Rites and rituals, totems and taboos and the culture and traditions of Jharkhand tribal women have also been taken into account.

My tribal inheritance made is easier to gather the data, which is mostly of my own and also collected by me through friends, relatives and acquaintances, who are leading an actual village life and are associated with forests. Totems and taboos have been explored through verbal communication with older generation. Interviews were carried out with tribal *baidyas*, *Pradhans* and village elders for gathering information regarding medicinal plants and herbal treatment practiced by tribal's *Horopathy*. Grandma's recipe of domestic treatment was also sought out. Some data was gathered from books and journals. Beautiful folklores in *Mundari, Santhali, Kurukh, Ho,* and *Kharia* were collected from books written in these specific languages by wise poets and authors. This pluralistic data becomes alive when looked from the perspective of the tribal women, and it becomes difficult to fix it as per precise scientific functions. Hence, whenever necessary, some *Mundari* words are added for more appropriate and specific explanation.

The word 'seasonal' is mentioned repeatedly because a season is of utmost importance to a tribal life. They do not do anything randomly or arbitrarily. There is an affixed time for every activity, that is, a season to cut timber woods, collect fire woods, to pluck leaves, to uproot tubers and even to gather grasses. A careful investigation of these activities will reveal scientific causes behind the fixed curriculum for each season. One can say that tribal life is marked by a rhythm that it inherits from nature and seamlessly incorporates in all aspects of its activities.

The study is logical and scientific based on the negotiations, research, and facts. Without any pride and prejudice, the book encapsulates true life pattern of a tribal woman to give her the lost glory and dignity as well as to preserve her intellect and knowledge for the welfare of mankind.

I hope the book will be beneficial to all those people who are eager to know about the biodiversity and ethnobotany of Jharkand and to understand the plant human relationship especially in context to indigenous women. The book may also be read as a small gesture of respect and admiration for the beautiful balance with nature that the tribal life represents and a balance that we are desperately trying to maintain in this age of rampant growth and industrialization.

Prabhawati Bodra

Acknowledgements

- I owe my gratitude and sincere thanks to all those who have helped and assisted me in various aspects of the book as without their help the book would not be in its present form.
- To Prof. (Dr.) K.K. Nag, Former Vice Chancellor, Ranchi University, Ranchi; Tilka Manjhi Bhagalpur University; Vinoba Bhave University, Hazaribagh for sparing his valuable time for writing the Foreword of the book.
- To Dr. Promodini Hansdak, Head of Department, P.G. Department of Hindi and Former Pro-Vice Chancellor, S.K.M. University, Dumka, for her encouragement.
- To Prof. (Dr.) Ashok Kumar Chaudhary, Director, Human Resource Development Centre, Ranchi University, Ranchi, for valuable suggestions.
- To Rev. T.S.C. Hans, Ranchi, for giving his valuable suggestions for the Mundari folklores and support in every aspect.
- To Shri Vijay Tudu, Ex-Secretary, Gota Bharot Sido Kanhu Hul Baisi, Dumka, for translating the Santhali folklores and sparing his valuable time whenever I needed his assistance for understanding the songs.
- To Dr. Mary Hansda, Assistant Professor, Department of Hindi, Presidency College, Kolkata for helping me with the selection of Santhali folklores.
- To Dr. Achyut Chetan, Assistant Professor, Department of English, S.P. College, Dumka, for his suggestion in vocabulary.

- To Prof. Poonam Binjha, Assistant Professor, Department of Economics, S.P. College, Dumka, for the translation of Kurukh folklores.
- Fr. James Lakra, Ex-Principal, St. Xavier's College, Maharo, Dumka for correcting the Kurukh vocabulary.
- To Dr. Damyanti Sinku, Department of Tribal and Regional Languages, Ranchi University, Ranchi for providing HO folklores and for translating it in Hindi.
- To Rev. George Santiel Kerketta, Gossner Theological College, Ranchi regarding Kharia folklores.
- To Fr. Emmanuel Baxla, In-charge, Fr. Camille Bulcke Research Centre, Ranchi, for providing library facility.
- To Mrs. Irene Demta, Mrs. Parakhlata Samad, Principal, Miss Baker Memorial Girl's High School and Villagers of Maranghada for introducing the biodiversity of the forest to me.
- To my sons, Pretish and Saurav, for their constant support and encouragement.
- To Ms. Tanaya Saha, Founder and Editor-in-Chief, Pen Friend, for proof reading and formatting the manuscript.

Contents

Abbreviations

E : English
H : Hindi
B : Bengali
M : Mundari
S : Santhali
Ku : Kurukh
N : Nagruria
V.N. : Vernacular Names

List of Plates

Introduction

The particular word "Abuá Bir" signifies the deep relationship of tribal woman with nature. If she denotes the forest as "our" meaning "their own", it is not in terms of any sort of claim, property rights or legal aspects. It only expresses her feeling of oneness, intimacy, and compassion for nature. This expression is not false; it comes from deep inside her heart, as the relationship between the two is nurtured by respect for community values and refined natural instincts.

The life of a tribal woman is centred on the forest and is the support-system of her life. The forest is like a faithful companion who fulfils her desire for the wellness of the family because it is the supplier of basic necessities of life in terms of food, fodder, fuel, medicine, gums, resins etc. The tribal woman efficiently plays the role of a wise natural resource manager and has the native talent of managing the forest resources accordingly for her best utilization.

Forest is a resource of sustainable livelihood for the tribal community. A tribal woman is a thoughtful economic counsellor who takes advantage of using the forest commodities for her economic liberty. Every element in the forest has a precisely defined value for her and she creatively utilizes it by developing an organic co-existence with it rather than a relation of utility. Seasonal collection and selling of non-timber forest produces is a common feature for self-sustainability of a tribal woman.

She is a natural scientist and an exemplary conserver of plant species. She collects and grows many plants in her home garden, *Bakhre.*[1] She is the cultivator and domesticator of many wild species. Timely collection, quality-wise grading, safe storage of seeds are some of her responsibilities. It is her natural habit to share and exchange seeds, tubers, saplings, etc. Even if she goes to other villages on some occasion, her interest in exploring new varieties of plants never ceases. *"Chala, bon, bhule jab"*, that is, "Come, let us go to the forest to roam about" is a common word of a guest woman to her friends and hostess. Thus, she is a protector and preserver of plant genetic species.

She has the traditional knowledge of herbal medicines and has proficient knowledge about the local flora. She knows the treatment of bruises, cuts, wounds, scorpion stings, insect crawl, snake bite, etc. because she encounters all these in the forest. Small ailments of cough, cold, fever, etc. are treated by her at home. She acts as a knowledgeable person who cares for the health of her family members. Some tribal women are also professionals of some specific diseases. They are called "*buid - era*"[2], a native medicine woman.

The moral, religious, social, and cultural traditions of tribal society are linked with nature. All these traditional knowledge are inherited by a tribal girl from her mother, grandmother, kith and kin. Since childhood she grows up learning about all the customs and rituals in a simple and natural way, so she is groomed to become a wise tribal woman who is well versed with nature.

She is custodian of social right and rituals and so practices the social totems and taboos. Forest flora aids her in performing all her social and cultural duties. She is a lifetime learner as well as teacher whose duty is to pass her inherited knowledge to the younger generation. Being a role model of tribal people, she expresses her feelings in songs, dances, stories, and folklores. These expressions of the tribal woman—some of which collected in this book—are a veritable resource for our understanding of the sentimental relation that the tribal woman has with every component of her habitat. These have come down to us orally through successive generations and have acted as the repository for the continuation of tribal life and their traditional identity for centuries. Most importantly, they are the unparallelled resources of the collective creativity of the tribal women.

Unfortunately, her knowledge and intelligence is totally ignored. the world is busy making decisions for her, but has totally disregarded her. It is time to project her life pattern in the forest based economy for both economical and environmental gain and to utilize her knowledge and experience in the future development programme especially in the tribal areas to stop migration and to provide sustenance. The book encapsulates the prominence of the tribal woman and addresses the ubiquitous presence of a tribal woman in society which needs greater acknowledgement and respect in the contemporary circumstances.

Notes

1. Encyelopaedia Mundarica – Rev. J. Hoffmann, Vol. 2, Page 341.
2. Encyelopaedia Mundarica – Rev. J. Hoffmann, Vol. 2, Page 329.

1
Forest Flora
Way of Sustenance of Tribal Woman

Forest is the repository of endless usage for tribal community. A tribal woman is well acquainted with the forest flora. The seasonal availability and variability of the forest species remains registered in her mind. She knows when, what and how to procure necessary things from the forest to satisfy all her needs. Forest is her food basket. Every season she picks up edibles in the form of fruits, flowers, floral buds, seeds, kernels, leaves, pot herbs, yams, roots, and tubers. Species yielding oil, gums, resins, ropes, dyes, latex, etc. are also timely harvested by her. Fuel wood for cooking and fodder for cattle are collected throughout the year from the forest. Special species are used as soaps, and ashcs of plants are prepared to be used as detergent to clean the cotton clothes. A tribal woman is well aware of the medicinal properties of the forest species and uses it for the treatment of small ailments at home. Twigs of shrubs are collected from the forest for making various articles of domestic usage. Variety of grasses and reeds are collected for making brooms, mats, etc. Most of the requirements are fulfilled by non-timber forest products (NTFPs). The pattern of getting the full utility and potentiality of forest species is practiced by her in many ways.

She uses the forest flora for her sustenance mainly in two ways.

"Nam Jom"[1]: Search for One's Own Use

In every season, a tribal woman collects various types of edibles from the forest. The young tender leaves, flowers, fruits, pot herbs, yams, tubers, etc. are collected in due time. A tribal woman is the caretaker of her family, so it is her responsibility to gather the forest products for feeding her family. It is a year long process and a tedious task which takes lots of time and energy, but she fulfils her duty and often enjoys it. Not only the poor but also the affluent village tribal women have a natural hobby of visiting the forest for gathering food articles though not on regular basis. Each season brings with it new forest products, and it is a joy for both rich and poor women to gather these new products. The only difference is that the poor sell it for their livelihood and to earn some money.

In a tribal home, the edibles collected from the forest are cooked everyday. The arrival of new edibles in the *thali* (food plate) also marks the onset and welcome of a new season. For example, in January, the purple flowers of "Jirhul"—*Indigofera pulchella* Roxb—are plucked from the forest and cooked. In summer, children relish the delicious "Kend"—*Diospyrus melanoxylon* Roxb—and the rain brings along with it the nutritive mushrooms (more examples in Table 1.2). Thus, the forest flora adds to the diet and so gathering these products is the responsibility of the lady of the house, as she is most concerned about the health and nutrition of the family, therefore, takes all the pain to fulfill her responsibility.

Necessary items of day-to-day use are procured by her from the forest. For example, species, yielding oil, gums, resins, dyes are searched and collected. Bamboos, grasses, and leaves are gathered for weaving mats, baskets, and for making brooms, etc.

Timing to Go to the Forest

A woman cannot go to the forest any time. The scorching sun, heavy rainfall, hale and storm inhibit her daily round to the forest. Apart from these natural calamities, there are some tribal taboos which she obeys as society's norms.

The Tribal Taboos

- A tribal woman avoids going to the forest in cloudy weather as it is believed that in such weather tigers, leopards, bear and wild animals come out of their hides even during the daytime in search of prey.

- In rainy season, hail and storms, she cannot go to the forest.
- A woman does not go to the forest all alone but in groups at least of two.
- They don't go in the lonely afternoons, as according to tribal saying, evil spirits roam about in the loneliness of the hour in the forest.
- Pregnant women are advised to avoid specific places, as it is believed that she will be shadowed more easily by the evil spirits in her condition.
- The best time considered for going to the forest is from morning till afternoon.

"Nam Udam"[2]: Search for Livelihood

Gathering of edibles and other utility items and earning a living by selling it is an age-old tradition in the tribal community. The art of earning livelihood by this traditional method is so ancient that it has been given a traditional name—"Nam Udam", that is, to earn a living by selling jungle or any other natural product. It is not only a way of earning livelihood by gathering and selling the forest produces, but it has also become a culture. It is not occasional but year long process of small income.

The direct use value is derived from the interaction of plant resources. These values are directly linked with the assessment of financial gain. The forest products may be called "green wealth" because these are continuous sources of small but steady income. The forest produces be it edibles or items of daily usage are collected and sold in the nearby village market (*bazaar*, *haat* or *haatiya*). These village markets are mostly held on weekly or bi-weekly basis. It is a general practice that tribal males, though few in number, sell timber wood, fuel woods, meat or fishes. The sight of tribal women selling their collected forest produces is not uncommon in tribal areas, rather more number of females are seen selling their forest utility items like pot herbs, edible leaves, fruits from the forest, etc. The dried variety of pot herbs and tender leaves fetch more money than the raw ones. Special forest resources, such as mushrooms, which grow in the monsoon, fetch good money because they are used as delicacies. Usually cultivated vegetables are not sold in the market unless produced in excess and are surplus after domestic use. The seasonal forest products are mainly collected and sold for twelve months in the local village market. Her relentless labour does not go in vain, as the small income fulfils her daily needs. Though the amount fetched through selling of products is small, it is a steady source of income for her. The forest acts like a mini bank by fulfilling her desires as well as providing assistance during adversity, sickness, and death. One can say that in all walks of life forest is her economic asset.

The salient feature of this labour is that the money is solely her own and she can use the amount according to her wish. The tribal community respects her labour and generally does not claim the money she gets by collecting and selling of the forest products. The autonomous economic activity of a tribal woman is indeed quite harmoniously in balance with her great sense of collective responsibility. The tribal woman retains her individuality and autonomy while being fully aware of her collective self. It is a marvellous example of the co-existence of values of solidarity and individuality which is an incredible social formation.

Enlistment of Forest Resources and Its Direct Use Value

The recorded forest area of Jharkhand state is 23,605 sq. km which is 29.61 per cent of the total geographical area. *(Forest Survey of India, 2011.)*

The depletion of forests has lead to severe unavailability of plants species, but a tribal woman still explores the forest in search of edibles and other utility items for her home and for selling in the market for money. Thus, the tribal concept of "Nam Jom" and "Nam Udam" is still practiced and fulfilled by her.

Some season-wise available forest resources are enlisted below. These are some of the common commodities collected and used at home as well as sold in the village market and nearby town. (See Table 1.1)

"Jogao Jaton"[3]: Wise Preservation by Tribal Woman

The tribal taboos, harsh weather, unavailability of forest food in certain months of the year have made it mandatory for the tribal woman to learn the art of preservation of the forest products.

Table 1.1: Direct Use Valued forest Resource per Season: Self Consumed and Saleable

Collection Time: January to March			
Botanical Name	**Vernacular Name**	**Family**	**Parts Used**
Bauhinia purpurea L.	Koinar	Caesalpiniaceae	Flowers
Centella asiatica L.	Bengsag	Apiaceae	Pot herb
Dillenia pentagyna Roxb.	Rai	Dilleniaceae	Fruits
Emblica officinalis Gartn.	Amla	Euphorbiaceae	Fruits
Ficus infectoria Roxb.	Putkal	Moraceae	Leaf buds
Ficus religiosa L.	Pipal	Moraceae	Young leaves
Ficus racemosa L.	Gular	Moraceae	Fruits
Ficus rumphii Blume.	Pakur	Moraceae	Fruits
Ficus semicordata Buch-Ham.	Jagya dumar	Moraceae	Green fruits, vegetables Ripe fruits, edible
Iindigofera pulchella Roxb.	Jirhul	Papilionaceae	Flowers
Limnophila conferta Benth.	Muchri sag	Scrophulariaceae	Pot herb
Marsilea minuta L.	Sunsunia sag	Marsileaceae	Pot herb
Oxalis corniculata L.	Katibuti	Oxalidaceae	Leaves
Vangueria pubescens Kurz.	Katai sag	Rubiaceae	Leaves
Zizyphus jujuba L.	Ber	Rhamnaceae	Fruits
Zizyphus oenoplia L.	Bir Janum	Rhamnaceae	Fruits

(*Contd.*)

Botanical Name	Vernacular Name	Family	Parts Used
Collection Time: April to June			
Botanical Name	**Vernacular Name**	**Family**	**Parts Used**
Aegle marmelos Correa.	Bel	Rutaceae	Fruits
Alternanthera sessilis Br.	Garundi ara	Amaranthaceae	Leaves
Amaranthus viridis L.	Jangli chaulai	Amaranthaceae	Leaves
Annona squamosa L.	Sarifa	Annonaceae	Fruits
Anogeissus latifolia Wall.	Hesel	Combretaceae	Fruits
Antidesma diandrum Roth.	Matta ara	Euphorbiaceae	Leaves
Artocarpus lakoocha Roxb.	Dahu	Moraceae	Fruits
Azadiracta indica Juss.	Neem	Meliaceae	Leaves
Bauhinia purpurea L.	Koinar sag	Caesalpiniaceae	Tender leaves
Bauhinia vahlii W & A.	Gungu	Caesalpiniaceae	Fried Seed
Buchanania lanzan Spreng.	Chironji	Anacardiaceae	Fruits, Seeds
Butea parviflora Roxb.	Baindu nari	Papilionaceae	Seeds
Diospyrus melanoxylon Roxb.	Kend	Ebenaceae	Fruits
Diospyrus montana Roxb.	Gada tiril	Ebenaceae	Fruits
Ficus glomerata Roxb.	Dumar	Moraceae	Fruits
Ficus macrophylla Roxb.	Kota	Moraceae	Fruits
Flacourtia indica Burm.	Merlec	Flacurtiaceae	Fruits
Ficus cunia Ham.	Hor Podo	Moraceae	Fruits
Limnophila conferata Benth.	Muchri Sag	Scrophulariaceae	Pot herb

(*Contd.*)

Botanical Name	Vernacular Name	Family	Parts Used
Madhuca indica Gmel.	Mahua	Sapotaceae	Leaf – Biri Fruits – Edible Seeds – Oil
Mangifera indica L.	Aam	Anacardiaceae	Fruits
Mucuna pruriens L.	Alkusi	Papilionaceae	Tender Leaves
Phoenix sylvestris Roxb.	Jangli Khajur	Arecaceae	Fruits
Polygonum plebejum Br.	Mui ara	Polygonaceae	Leaves
Scirpus grossus L.	Kesair	Cyperaceae	Tubers
Semecarpus anacardium L.	Bhelwa	Anacardiaceae	Fruits
Shorea robusta Gaertn.	Sal	Dipterocarpaceae	Fruits
Syzygium cuminii L.	Jamun	Myrtaceae	Fruits
Syzygium heyneana Wall.	Kat jamun	Myrtaceae	Fruits
Tamarindus indica L.	Imli	Caesalpiniaceae	Tender leaves, Fruits, Cotyledon
Terminalia bellerica Roxb.	Behra	Combretaceae	Fruits
Terminalia Chebula Retz.	Harra	Combretaceae	Fruits
Ziziphus rugosa Lamk.	Sirka	Rhamnaceae	Fruits

Collection Time: July to September

Botanical Name	Vernacular Name	Family	Parts Used
Agaricus sp.	Mushroom	Agaricaceae	Fruiting body
Antidesma ghaesembilla Gaertn.	Mata sura	Euphorbiaceae	Fruits

(*Contd.*)

Botanical Name	Vernacular Name	Family	Parts Used
Boerhaavia diffusa L.	Khapra sag	Nyctaginaceae	Leaves
Carissa carandas L.	Karaunda	Apocynaceae	Fruits
Celosia argentea L.	Sirgiti ara	Amaranthaceae	Pot herb
Cleome monophylla L.	Hurhuria ara	Cappariaceae	Pot herb
Dioscorea aculeata L.	Tungam sanga	Dioscoreaceae	Tubers
Dendrocalamus strictus Nees.	Bans	Poaceae	Young culms
Gardenia gummifera L.	Bururi	Rubiaceae	Fruits
Leucas cephalotes Roth.	Guma ara	Labiatae	Pot herb
Lycoperdon sp.	Rugra	Lycoperdaceae	Fruiting body
Schleichera oleosa Lour.	Kusum	Sapindaceae	Fruit, seed-oil
Syzygium cuminii L.	Jamun	Myrtaceae	Fruits
Syzygium heymeana Wall.	Kat Jamun	Myrtaceae	Fruits
Solena heterophylla Lour.	Bir Kundri	Cucurbitaceae	Tender leaves, Fruits
Spondias pinnata L.	Ambra	Anacardiaceae	Fruits

Collection Time: October to December

Botanical Name	Vernacular Name	Family	Parts Used
Bauhinia vahlii W & A.	Gungu	Caesalpiniaceae	Seeds
Cassia tora L.	Chakor	Caesalpiniaceae	Tender leaves
Celastrus paniculata Wild.	Kujri	Celastraceae	Fruits-Oil
Dioscorea bulbifera L.	Harad bo	Dioscoreaceae	Rhizomes

(*Contd.*)

Botanical Name	Vernacular Name	Family	Parts Used
Dioscorea glabra Roxb.	Unur sanga	Dioscoreaceae	Tubers
Dioscorea alata Roxb.	Buru sanga	Dioscoreaceae	Tubers
Dioscorea belophylla Roxb.	Hasa sanga	Dioscoreaceae	Tubers
Dioscorea anguina Roxb.	Kukuri sanga	Dioscoreaceae	Tubers
Dioscorea pentaphylla L.	Hesor sanga	Dioscoreaceae	Tubers
Flacourtia cataphracta Roxb.	Paniyara	Flacourtiaceae	Fruits
Flacourtia indica Burm.	Merlec	Flacourtiaceae	Fruits
Gardinia latifolia A & H.	Papara	Rubiaceae	Fruits
Momordica dioica Roxb.	Ochen/Ban Khaksi	Cucurbitaceae	Tender Leaves and Fruits
Mucuna nivea D.C.	Kursa	Fabaceae	Seeds
Olax scandens Roxb.	Rimil biri	Olacaceae	Tender Leaves and Fruits
Plesmonium margaritiferum Schott.	Bir Hada	Araceae	Tubers
Phaseolus calcaratus Roxb.	Bir sutra	Papilionaceae	Seeds
Portulaca oleracea L.	Dail ara/golgola sag	Portulacaceae	Pot herb
Panicum crus-galli L.	Sama ghas	Poeaceae	Seeds
Psidium guajava L.	Tamras/Amrud	Myrtaceae	Fruits
Spondias pinnata L.	Amra	Anacardiaceae	Fruits
Solanum nigrum L.	Buru diang	Solanaceae	Fruits
Zizyphus oenoplia Mill.	Kudi rama	Rhamnaceae	Fruits

It is here essential to bring to notice that during summer in Jharkhand, it is very difficult to cultivate vegetables because of the scarcity of water and irrigation facilities. The yield of vegetables grown in the fields, *Bari* or *Bakhre*, is very less. *Bari* or *Bakhre* is a fenced plot of land behind a house where generally vegetables are grown. Green vegetables are available in the market but the prices are so high in summer that it is beyond the reach of poor tribal people.

At the same time, pot herbs and leaves which are picked up as edible commodities from the forest also perish owing to summer heat. Hence, the availability of fresh vegetables in the home garden and edible herbs in the forest becomes inadequate and meagre. To combat such adverse situation, the tribal woman has learnt the art of preservation from time immemorial. She collects the pot herbs and green leaves when it is easily accessible. The fresh articles are then preserved through the unique process of cleaning, drying, and storing in a very uncommon and healthy way. These dried items are used during summer as a substitute to green vegetables.

Significance

The species commonly selected for preservation is said to contain high vitamin content and minerals. These species have been added since ages in the indigenous food habit keeping in mind its medicinal properties. It helps to fight malnutrition and many diseases. Economically and socially it helps in surviving the hard summer months when fresh vegetables are scarce and little rice is at home.

The Unique Tribal Way of Preservation Maintained by Women

The whole process of preservation is done in a special and unique method of processing which is described step by step below:

1. Time of Collection

The seasonal collection of herbs, leaves, etc. varies accordingly from species to species. Many of them are collected when they are tender and not very mature. For example, the leaves of "tamarind"—*Tamarindus indica* L.—are collected when they are new and tender and bear a distinct parrot green colour. The leaves of "katai"—*Vangueria pubescens* Kurz.—are collected in mature stage after winter season because it is said that the leaves of "katai" that undergo cold winter are tastier and nutritive. Likewise the leaves of "chakor"—*Cassia tora* L.—are collected in its flowering stage and not before or after. Hence, it is clear that the method of collection is not at all random rather it follows a certain tradition.

2. Cleaning and Drying

The collected items are manually cleaned, washed, and simply sundried just enough to make it crunchy. Some are given just a boil in water and then put in artifacts made of bamboo strips such as *Soop, Daura, Dalia,* etc., because these facilitate good aeration which is most necessary in the whole process of drying. The colour of the dried material is to be strictly maintained.

The leaves should not be dried for long because it should retain the green colour; severe drying of these leaves may change the colour of the dried material from green to brown. This is considered as a disqualification. The maintained green colour enhances its nutritive value.

3. Pounding

The dried material is hand pounded and coarsely powdered.

4. Storage

Sakam Potom – A unique structure is made up of stitched leaves usually of "*Sal*"—*Shorea robusta* Gaertn.—leaf, which is made by women to preserve the powdered items or dried items. After storing the pounded stuff, the women stitch it again to give it a ball like structure which is called *potom*. This is never opened. A hole big enough to insert the fingers inside it to take out the preserved stuff is made and through that hole the stuff is taken out. These *potoms* are hanged in the kitchen where food is cooked on traditional firewood—*chulha* (stove). These stuffs thus preserved remain fresh and free from moisture the whole year. In the next collecting season, these are renewed, as the old preserved item are discouraged and considered not fit and tasty for consumption.

However, certain taboos are made and followed for utilizing the preserved stuff. It is advised to take out the stuff with a clean and dried hand. Moreover, women having menstrual period should not touch the *potom*.

Methods of Preparation

The dried stuff is prepared following a simple method without destroying its nutritive and medicinal values. During summer, it is just fried with small amount of oil or without oil and starchy water of boiled rice is added to it. This recipe is called *Mandh jhor,* which is supposed to give a cooling effect to the body. It is stomach filling with many medicinal properties.

Table 1.2: Some Plants Species Popularly Selected for Storage in *Potoms*

Sl. No.	*Botanical Name*	*Vernacular Name*	*Family*	*Parts Used*
1.	*Centella asiatica* L.	Beng Sag	Apiaceae	Whole plant
2.	*Ficus infectoria* Roxb.	Putkal	Moraceae	New Leaf buds
3.	*Cassia tora* L.	Chakor	Caesalpiniaceae	Mature Leaves
4.	*Vangueria pubescens* Kurz.	Katai Sag	Rubiaceae	Mature Leaves
5.	*Mangifera indica* L.	Aam	Anacardiaceae	(Unripe and green fruits)
6.	*Moringa oleifera* Lam.	Munga	Moringaceae	Tender Leaves
7.	*Tamarindus indica* L.	Imli	Caesalpiniaceae	Tender Leaves
8.	*Tamarindus indica* L.	Imli	Caesalpiniaceae	Deseeded ripe Fruits
9.	*Emblica officinalis* Gaertn.	Amla	Euphorbiaceae	Fruits
10.	*Solanum tuberosum* L.	Alu sag	Solanaceae	Leaves
11.	*Ipomea batatas* Lamk.	Kanda Sag	Solanaceae	Leaves
12.	*Hibiscus sabdariffa* L.	Kudrum	Malvaceae	Red calyx

Notes

1. *Mundari Dictionary*, Dr. M. M. Mundu, p. 527.
2. *Ibid*.
3. *Ibid*.

2

Forest Flora

A Herbal Clinic of Tribal Woman

Decades back the villages of Jharkhand were surrounded by dense forests and deep rivers with little approach to urbanization. An innate relationship prevailed between residing communities and nature with their dependency on health care issues along with some basic requirements. Native flora and fauna are utilized for their curative properties, so forest acts as a cornucopia of herbal resources. Innumerable varieties of roots, stolons, bulbs, leaves, etc., were valued for their medicinal uses. More research is required to assemble information about the ways in which the natives gather the knowledge related to usage of plant resources as traditional drug. However, a secret and sacred therapy existed in the whole forest region which was later on classified as *Horopathy.* It may be thus termed as an ancient way of herbal remediation practised by the indigenous community of Jharkhand. Certainly a school of phytotherapy, one can say. Although every adult tribal was supposed to know the remedy of one or other common ailment, some people mastered the ancient art. These people were known as *baidhaya, baid, kaviraj* etc. In *Mundari,* they are called as *baid, buid or buidi.* In Santhal Pargana, they are known as *raranić,* that is, the medicine man. The traditional healers were experts in their respective field and had the meticulous knowledge of medicinal properties of wild plants. In the whole process of remediation, forest acts as a store house of medicinal plants, a natural repository of traditional medicine, a herbal clinic or herbal pharmacy. Precise knowledge of herbs, proper time and quantity of collection, method of preparation of medicine, proper diagnosis and exact doses were some of the features observed and practised minutely by the *baidhayas*.

This ancient method of remediation is not totally a thing of past but is still prevalent in the villages though to a much lesser extent. The present easy approach to allelopathic treatment, unavailability of expert herbal practitioners, deforestation and loss of vegetation including medicinal plants are some of the reasons in the present scenario of the slow death of this invaluable art.

It is necessary to bring to focus that whatsoever may be the reason, the herbal practitioners were and are mostly males, and the dominion of herbal practice was supposed to be a male's jurisdiction.

The method of ancient remediation can be studied under two subheadings[1]:

(a) Sećakan Buid-era: A specialized native medicine woman
(b) Kasec'akan ranun: Unspecialized ethno medicinal practices

Sećakan Buid-Era: A Specialized Native Medicine Woman

Sećakan buid-era is a term in *Mundari* meaning a specialized native medicine woman. As said earlier, herbal practice is generally in the hands of male herbal healers but some tribal women are experts in herbal remediation in a specific field. They are not to be confused with village women who act as midwives and assist in child birth and pre- and post-natal care. A *buid-era* is a female herbal physician who is generally specialized in one specific disease and people suffering from that particular disease go to her for cure. The difference with their male counterparts is that a male *baidhaya* knows the treatment of many ailments be it common or severe, whereas the female *buid-era* is mainly expertise in a single field of therapy. They are not exactly professionals like male *baidhayas* who may go to the patient's home in the same village or other, rather the female medicine women generally stay at home and her patients from far and near come to her house seeking for treatment. The medicines used are of course herbal which are gathered mostly from the forest. Many types of herbs, roots, barks, shoots from the forest are collected and fried in different oil in slow fire for the preparation of medicinal oil.

Some of the Specific Diseases Practised by *Buid-Erás*

1. Dental Problem

Some *buid-erás* are famous for their treatment of dental care. They know the herbal treatment of toothache, gum troubles, etc. They call their patients in empty stomach, early in the morning and treat them accordingly. Though they do not disclose their way of treatment, but it is studied that "Rangaini"—*Solanum xanthocarpum* Schrad—is one of the ingredients of the medicine they use for dental care.

2. Jaundice: Disorder of Liver

Some *buid-erás* are experts for the treatment of jaundice. Perfect diagnosis and identification is done by her. She makes pills or doses from freshly grinded leaves and roots of plants. Grinding is done by hand in a stone grinder. The medicine is never stale and is freshly prepared before the arrival of the patients. The patients receive their doses early morning in empty stomach before breakfast. The doses are given to the patients according to the severity of the disease. General dose is thrice a week but can be continued for a month based on the case. Instructions for the daily routine of life given by her include specific diet, less work-load, and non-consumption of alcohol. It should be strictly followed for better result and complete cure.

3. Paediatric Problem

Rangbad and Puni are common problems of a new born and are treated by *buid-erás* who are specialized in these paediatric problems.

Rangbad is the allergy in the mouth of new born babies. The inner part of the mouth and tongue turns red and irritation persists. The baby cannot suck mother's milk. The female practitioner gives a cream made of herbal plants to put inside the mouth. The cream is edible, safe and does not harm the infant. Instructions are given to the mother to consume bland diet and to avoid spices, brinjals, chilli etc.

Puni is the weakness of bones of infants. The small babies suffering from weak bones have the habit of crossing their legs (*kainchi paun* or scissor legs). Herbal massage oil is given to strengthen the weak bones.

4. Gynaecological Disorder

Disorders like infertility, miscarriage, painful menstruation, leucorrhea are cured by the herbal treatment of *buid-erás*. The method of abortion is not considered good by them and so most of them do not give medicine for it.

Kasećakan Ranun: Unspecialized Ethno-medicinal Practices

The tough life pattern of tribal women is such that for the safety of herself and for her family she must know the medicinal properties of the plants of the forest vegetation or local flora. A tribal woman has to work hard for her survival. It is a daily task for her to go to the forest to gather fuel, fodder, fruits, pots herbs, etc. Climbing trees, going through thorny bushes, ascending the cliff, passing through mud, streams and slopes to collect forest produces is her routine procedure. In this process, her body receives cuts, bruises, wounds, allergy caused by insect crawl, etc. She may suffer from honeybee sting, insect sting, scorpion sting, and even snake bite. Treatment of these casualties on the spot then and there is a must. Delaying the treatment may be fatal and may even cause life risk. Therefore, the primary treatment of all these casualties is a must which makes it crucial for these tribal women to have the knowledge related to curing of these harms through the medicinal plants of the forest. These treatments are simple and easy. Hence, for her own safety and her fellow-mates, a tribal woman must have the knowledge to identify the medicinal plants and know its properties for cure. This ethno-medicinal knowledge is acquired by her from her mother, grandmother, and ancestors; she uses the traditional ethno-medicinal knowledge for her cure and survival. It may be remarked that like the aesthetic values that eloquently present themselves in their songs, even these specialised forms of knowledge percolate down to these tribal women through close, intra- and inter-generational bonds with each other.

Method of Treatment

In a forest, providing aid for casualties cannot be sophisticated. It is done by simple and quick method of making medicine by extraction of juices and coarse grinding of herbs into pastes which is applied to the victim externally or orally or both as the case require.

The Procedure for Making Herbal Medicine is as follows:

Extraction of Plant Juices

The juices of leaves and plants are generally applied in cuts and wounds. For extraction of juices, the leaves and herbs are rubbed vigorously in between the palms of the two hands and squeezed; no water is added. The juice extracted is fresh and pure.

Making Paste of Plant Leaves

For making paste on the spot, the herbal plants are grinded coarsely in some rock with a stone. Mostly adding water is avoided to maintain the purity and quality of the paste.

In context to the place of occurrence and type of ailments, the traditional medication can be categorised into two:

1. *Roka ranun*: Instant remediation
2. *Orá re ranun*: Home remedies

Roka[2] Ranun[3]: Instant Remediation

The meaning of *roka ranun* in Mundari is instant remediation. As already described, women are the main collectors of almost all basic requirements of life from the forest. In this context, they have to daily encounter numerous casualties that need to be treated spontaneously. She cannot afford to waste time by returning to the village. She has the inherited knowledge related to identifying the medicinal herbs and treating the victim accordingly.

Achyranthes aspera L. F: Amaranthaceae

Vernacular Name: E: Pricky chaff flower; H: Latjira; B: Apang; M, Ku: chirchiti; S: Kakṛalaṭha.

Habit and Stature: The herb is common and it grows throughout the year. It is erect and subscandent. The fruit contains a single seed, and is indehiscent. It easily sticks to the coat of animals and clothes of human being. A plant of much importance in tribal medicine.

Parts Used: Leaves

Ethnomedicinal Uses: Juice from leaves are extracted and applied externally in the case of scorpion sting.

Andrographis echioides Nees. F: Acanthaceae

Vernacular Names: M: Gusum puru; S: Bir-kubet, Poshak; Ku: Nadnaur; N: Neola kanta.

Habit and Stature: It is an erect symmetrical herb with pubescent stems 8 inch to 2 ft high.

Parts Used: Whole plant.

Ethnomedicinal Uses: Whole plant is made into a paste and applied externally over wounds, cuts, boils and snake bite.

Aristolochia indica L. F: Aristolochiaceae

Vernacular Names: E: Indian birthwort; H, B: Isharmul; M: Nanri nagbail; S: Jhunką god′; N: Pagal ki jari.

Habit and Stature: This herb is common in open forests. It is a glabrous herbaceous or shrubby perennial with a woody root stalk which is extensively used in herbal medicines for mental disorder; hence the name is "Pagal ki jari."

Parts Used: Roots

Ethnomedicinal Uses: Root is made into powder form and applied in snake bite and scorpion sting.

Borreria hipsida L. F: Rubiaceae

Vernacular Names: H: Satgidhia; M, S: Hada pota.

Habit and Stature: It is a very common weed in open waste lands and pastures and is a procumbent scabrid or hispid herb much branched from the root.

Parts Used: Leaves

Ethnomedicinal Uses: Leaves are made into paste and applied externally in cuts and wounds.

Boerhaavia diffusa L. F: Nyctaginaceae

Vernacular Names: H: Punarva; M: Piri Kecho ará; S: Ohoć aṛaḱ; N: Khapra sag.

Habit and Stature: It is a pot herb that has many branches. It is perennial and grows throughout the year in waste grounds, fields, and road sides. The herb contains an alkaloid, Punarnavine. A diuretic, it promotes urination in case of dropsy.

Parts Used: Leaves

Ethnomedicinal Uses: Plant extract is used externally over wounds.

Careya arborea Roxb. F: Lecythidaceae

Vernacular Name: H, B: kumbi; M: Kindarkom; S: kumbir; Ku: kombi; N: kumbi.

Habit and Stature: It is a moderate sized tree that thrives in moist and shady region in the forests. Its old leaves are often red or purple in colour and it is deciduous at the time of flowering.

Parts Used: Leaves

Ethnomedicinal Uses: Juice of leaves is applied externally for nasal bleeding due to summer heat.

Cassia sophera L. F: Caesalpiniaceae

Vernacular Names: M: Marang chakonda; N: Barka chakonr.

Habit and Stature: It is an anthelmintic which is a stout shrub of 4 inch to 7 inch in height and is common in all districts.

Parts Used: Roots

Ethnomedicinal Uses: Root is made into a paste and is applied externally for treating snake bite and poison of insect crawl.

Cassine glauca Rott. F: Celastraceae

Vernacular Names: M: Nirsing; S: Ratan gaura.

Habit and Stature: It is an evergreen large tree which is very common in the foothills. The branch lets are reddish in colour and are dark red from inside, which exude a watery sap when cut. During summer when most of the tree leaves wilt, the leaves of this tree remains dark green. It is also cultivated as an ornamental tree.

Parts Used: Roots

Ethnomedicinal Uses: Root is made into a paste and applied on wounds caused by injury.

Cassia tora L. F: Caesalpiniaceae

Vernacular Names: H.B.: Chakund; M: Huring chakonda ará; S: Chakaoňa; Ku: Sani chakonda; N: chakor

Habit and Stature: It is an erect herb which is 1 inch to 5 inch in height. This herb is very common and sub gregarious which grows in waste ground and forest glades during the rainy season.

Parts Used: Leaves

Ethnomedicinal Uses: Leaves are made into paste and applied externally when stinged by honey bee, wasp, and other insects.

Clitoria ternatea L. F: Papilionaceae

Vernacular Name: E: Butterfly pea, Mussel shell creper; H, B: Aparajita; M: Saank ba; S: Ruhu tuhu.

Habit and Stature: It is a very beautiful slender twiner grows commonly in gardens and is largely cultivated as ornamental twining herb for its azure blue rarely pure white flowers. Flowers and seeds yield a blue dye.

Parts Used: Leaves

Ethnomedicinal Uses: Leaves are made into paste and applied externally on scorpion sting and snake bite. The juice extracted from leaves is given orally in both the above cases.

Commelina benghalensis L. F: Commelinaceae

Vernacular Names: H: Kanchara; M: Undupu ará; S: Kana aṛaḱ; Ku: Kenar arxa; N: Kena sag.

Habit and Stature: It is a small dichotomously branched diffused perennial pot herb that is found along ditches, streams and also in rice and vegetable fields. Leaves are sometimes used as vegetable.

Parts Used: Whole plant

Ethnomedicinal Uses: Plant is made into paste and applied externally on insect crawl and scorpion sting.

Crinum latifolium L. F: Amaryllidaceae

Vernacular Names: M: Kulac ba; S: Sikiyom baha; Ku, N: Kanai.

Habit and Stature: It is a beautiful species which gives flowers before the leaves are fully developed and bears 8-10 large white inclined or drooping flowers more or less tinged with rose colour along the centre of the tepals. This herb grows in dry jungles, often in the banks of river.

Parts Used: Leaves

Ethnomedicinal Uses: Juice from leaves is extracted and applied as drop for nasal bleeding caused by summer heat.

Curcuma amada Roxb. F: Zingiberaceae

Vernacular Names: E: Mango ginger; H: Amhaldi; M: Kead sanga; Ku: Bondo balka; N: Van haldi.

Habit and Stature: This herb is very common in the forests and the plant from root to tip is only 2 to 2.5 ft. and bears scape from the centre of the leafy tuff. The root stock is small and is pale yellow with white margings fibers ending in tubers. The fresh cut root stock has the smell of green mango and it is used as carminative and for cooling.

Parts Used: Tubers

Ethnomedicinal Uses: The paste of tubers is applied externally for spider poison, insect bite and insect crawl.

Cyperus rotundus L. F: Cyperaceae

Vernacular Names: E: Nut grass; H: Nagarmotha; B: Mutha; M: Piri jimtu; S: Muthạ ghãs N: Motha Ku: Motha ghansi.

Habit and Stature: It is a small and slender sedge arising from small hard corns or tubers or bearing tubers on its slender wiry stolons. The tubers have a pleasant fragrance and are about 0.5" in diameter ovoid, black or dark brown outside, white within.

Parts Used: Roots

Ethnomedicinal Uses: Roots paste is applied externally and also given orally to drink in case of scorpion sting.

Cynodon dactylon Pers F: Poaceae

Vernacular Names: E: The lawn grass, Bermuda grass, H: Dub ghas; B: Durba, M: Dubila tasad; S: Dhubi ghãs, N: Dubla ghans; Ku: Duba ghansi.

Habit and Stature: The plant grows mainly on sandy soil throughout the area. It is a rather variable creeping or ascending grass with stems widely spread and frequently matted.

Parts Used: Whole plant

Ethnomedicinal Uses: Plant paste is applied externally and also given orally to drink for curing scorpion sting and snake bite.

Emblica officinalis Gaertn F: Euphorbiaceae

Vernacular Names: E: Emblic myrabolan, Indian gooseberry; H: Amla; M, S: Meral; Ku: Anra; N: Aonra.

Habit and Stature: A small or moderate sized deciduous tree, which is common throughout the forest. The fruit is globose, succulent, yellow or pink when ripe. The fruit contains gallic acid and is astringent but sialagogue and hence is often taken by the villagers in the forest when thirsty. Fruit is astringent, antidiarrhoel, antidysentric, antiscorbutic, carmonative, cooling, stomachic, and tonic.

Parts Used: Fruits

Ethnomedicinal Uses: Fruit juice is applied externally and also given orally in case of scorpion sting.

Evolvulus nummularis L. F: Convolvulaceae

Vernacular Names: E: Dwarf morning glory; M: Piri choke lutur; S: Tanr sushni

Habit and Stature: It is a small prostrate herb that is usually found in open pasture land and dry banks.

Parts Used: Leaves

Ethnomedicinal Uses: Leaves juice is externally applied for curing scorpion sting.

Holarrhena antidysenterica Wall F: Apocynaceae

Vernacular Names: H, B: Koraiya, Kurchi; M: Toa baha; S: Haṭ baha; Ku: korkoria.

Habit and Stature: It is a large shrub or a small tree that is very common in the area. It grows frequently on the laterite. The shrub has sweet scented, white flowers, hence the Mundari named it '*toa baha*' which means like milk (white).

Parts Used: Flowers

Ethnomedicinal Uses: The flower is used for curing nasal bleeding.

Hyptis suaveolens L. F: Lamiaceae

Vernacular Names: E: Pignut or Chan; H, B: Bilaiti Tulsi; M: Dhangri nacha; S: Purodo; Dimbu baha.

Habit and Stature: It is a tall coarse, branched, very sweet smelling herb which grows naturally and is common in forests.

Parts Used: Leaves

Ethnomedicinal Uses: Leaves juice is used for curing nasal bleeding.

Litsaea polyantha Juss. F: Lauraceae.

Vernacular Names: H: Meda; B: Kukur chiota; M, S, K: Pojo.

Habit and Stature: It is a small evergreen tree found in valleys chiefly near streams.

Parts Used: Bark

Ethnomedicinal Uses: Paste of bark is applied externally in sprains and bruises.

Martynia annua L. F: Martyniaceae

Vernacular Names: E: Tiger's claws, Devil's claws; H: Baghanakhi; M: Bana sarsar; S: Bag lucã; Ku, N: Gaymukhi.

Habit and Stature: A shrub 3-4 ft high, clammy and pubescent. Thoroughly naturalised and found in all districts. The fruit when dehisced leaves a crustaceous sculptured endocarp with two sharp curved apical spines and a central channel opening between the spines, hence, in English it is named as Devil's claw or Tiger's claw. In Hindi, it is named Baghanakhi, that is, Tiger's claw.

Parts Used: Leaves

Ethnomedicinal Uses: Leaves juice is applied externally to cure wounds and to stop bleeding due to cuts. It is also applied externally in snake bite.

Mucuna nivea DC. F: Papilionaceae

Vernacular Names: M: Kursi; S, Ku, N: Kursa

Habit and Stature: It is a slendar climber that grows in the wild, and is sometimes cultivated.

Parts Used: Seeds

Ethnomedicinal Uses: For curing snake bite, paste of six seeds is given with water.

Murraya exotica L. F: Rutaceae

Vernacular Names: E: The Chinese myrtle, the white jasmine; H, B: Kamini; M: Atil sing; S: Aṭhel.

Habit and Stature: It is a much branched evergreen shrub or small tree that are frequent in the hills and in rocky ravines. The plant is commonly grown in gardens for its glossy green foliage and large cluster of fragrant white flowers. The corolla tubes yield an orange dye.

Parts Used: Leaves

Ethnomedicinal Uses: Powdered leaves or juice is used externally in fresh cuts.

Nyctanthes arbortristis L. F: Oleaceae

Vernacular Name: E: Night jasmine, Weeping nyctanthes; H: Harsingar; M: Saparom; S: Saparom; Ku: Seoli; N: Murjhatni.

Habit and Stature: It is a small tree common in the hills and rocky ravines. The flowers mainly grow in the month of September and October and have good fragnance. The flowers are white with orange tubes that open in the evening and drop next morning.

Parts Used: Leaves

Ethnomedicinal Uses: Leaves paste is given with water orally in snake bite.

Sida acuta *Burm. F: Malvaceae*

Vernacular Names: E: Wire weed; H: Bariar; M: Bir ipirpiung; S: Bir miru baha.

Habit and Stature: It is an erect herb or undershrub that is 2–3 ft high and commonly grows in the waste grounds. Stems are very tough and the plants are used as brooms in the villages.

Parts Used: Roots

Ethnomedicinal Uses: Root paste is applied externally in the case of scorpion sting.

Sida cordifolia L. F: Malvaceae

Vernacular Names: E: Country mallow; H: Bariar; B: Bala; M: Marang lupu ara; S: Laṭha chipchiṛiṕ.

Habit and Stature: It is an erect undershrub that is 2–4 ft high and commonly grows in the waste places throughout the area, especially in scrub forests.

Parts Used: Roots

Ethnomedicinal Uses: Paste of roots is applied externally for healing cuts and wounds.

Sida rhombifolia L. F: Malvaceae

Vernacular Names: E: Arrow leaf sida; H: Sah devi; M: Ipirpiung.

Habit and Stature: It is a herb or undershrub that is 1–4 ft. high and is very common in the waste ground, road sides, and forest glades.

Parts Used: Leaves

Ethnomedicinal Uses: Leaves paste is applied externally to cure wounds, cut, swelling, and sprains.

Tridax procumbens L. F: Asteraceae

Vernacular Names: H: Kharghos ghas; M: Hochod tasad; S: Jo̱rmo̱t aṛaḱ; Ku: Munya arxa; N: Kharha ghas.

Habit and Stature: It is a herb that is abundant in pastures, banks, waste ground, and forests. The most common and well recognized herb is very popular for instant remediation of cuts, wounds, etc., among the villagers.

Parts Used: Leaves

Ethnomedicinal Uses: Leaves juice and paste is applied externally in cuts, wounds, sprains. It also stops bleeding due to cuts.

Vernonia cinera L. F: Asteraceae

Vernacular Names: E: Purple fleabane, Ash coloured fleabane, Little iron weed; H: Sahadevi; B: Kalajeera; M: Pirimaga; S: Baṛangom.

Habit and Stature: It is very common, erect or somewhat document branched herb that is found in the whole area.

Parts Used: Whole plant parts

Ethnomedicinal Uses: Whole plant is made into a paste and applied on wounds.

Vitex peduncularis Wall. F: Verbenaceae

Vernacular Name: H, N: Charaigorwa; B: Boruna; M: Simkata, Marakata; Ku: Erutatka; S: Mará kaṭa.

Habit and Stature: It is an evergreen, small or moderate sized tree found in valleys or rocky slopes in the forest.

Parts Used: Bark

Ethnomedicinal Uses: Paste of the bark is made by mixing water that is applied externally in snake bite. Sometimes, it is also orally applied.

Zizyphus jujuba Lamk. F: Rhamnaceae

Vernacular Name: E: Jujube fruit; H: Baer; M: Dodari; S: Jom janum; Ku: Pan; N: Koir.

Habit and Stature: It is a small tree, common throughtout the area which is cultivated or self sown over the area. The fruit is eaten and it is believed that it purifies blood. The bark contains much tannin and is a remedy for diarrhoea.

Parts Used: Leaves

Ethnomedicinal Uses: Leaves paste is applied externally in case of insect bite and scorpion sting.

Orá[4] re ranun: Home Remedies

"Orá re ranun" is a Mundari word which means home remedies. The traditional knowledge of ethnomedicine is a great help for the treatment of common ailments at home. A tribal woman posseses this quality as she inherits the methods of treatment in a normal way from her grandmother and other ladies of the family. It is but natural that in the process of her growing up, she becomes well versed in the treatment of many simple diseases like cough and cold, fever, diahorrea, dysentery, headache etc. The society also expects a woman to have the talent to treat the ordinary ailments at home. A woman is well appreciated if she has this indigenous knowledge. Simple ailments are treated by the woman and other members of the family.

Some simple home remedies are given below:

COMMON COUGH AND COLD

Adhatoda vasica Nees. F: Acanthaceae

Vernacular Names: E: The Malabar nut; H: Adusa; B: Vasaka, Bokas; M: Arandi ba, Here ba; S: Basok; Ku, N: Bakaspati.

Habit and Stature: A wild bushy shrub that is common in or near the villages. Leaves and roots are considered good expectorant and anti-spasmodic and is used in phthisis.

Parts Used: Leaves

Ethnomedicinal Uses: The extract of leaves is mixed with honey and given twice or thrice daily. It loosens the thick sputum which comes out of throat giving relief in cough.

Curcuma longa L. F: Zingiberaceae

Vernacular Names: E: Turmeric; H: Haldi; B: Halud; M, S: Sasang; Ku: Balka; N: Hardi.

Habit and Stature: It is a perennial herb with tuberous rhizomes that is cultivated more or less in the whole area. Rhizome is of orange red colour and is used both as spice and medicine.

Parts Used: Rhizomes

Ethnomedicinal Uses: One teaspoon of turmeric powder is put in a cup of lukewarm milk and given to drink. It loosens the thick sputum and brings relief.

Moringa oleifera Lamk. F: Moringaceae

Vernacular Names: E: Drumstick, Horse radish; H: Sahjan; B: Sojna; M: Munga ará; S: Mungạ aṛaḱ; Ku: Munga arxa; N: Munga sag.

Habit and Stature: It is a small but wild tree that is usually cultivated in the whole area. The leaves, flowers, and fruits of the tree are eaten. The pungent root is used as vesicant and has the odour and flavour of horse radish, therefore, also used as a substitute.

Parts Used: Leaves

Ethnomedicinal Uses: A handful of fresh leaves is boiled in a litre of water till it is reduced to half and the colour of boiled water turns light yellow. This lukewarm decoction is taken in the morning as well as in the evening for cough and cold.

Spilanthes acmella Murr. F: Asteraceae

Vernacular Names: E: Toothache plant, electric daisy; M: Bocho topi.

Habit and Stature: It is a herb with long weak stems creeping at the base and is found in watery places but not very common in the area.

Parts Used: Flower heads

Ethnomedicinal Uses: Flower heads with sugar candy is taken in cough.

Terminalia bellerica Roxb. F: Combretaceae

Vernacular Names: E: Beleric myrabolan; H: Bahera; B: Bohera; M: Lupung; S: Loponġ; Ku, N: Bahra.

Habit and Stature: It is a large tree growing throughout the whole area, usually in Sal and mixed forests. It grows mostly in valleys and constitute of "triphala" (Aurvedic medicine) used in numerous diseases. The fruits are antibacterial and also rich in tannin.

Parts Used: Seeds

Ethnomedicinal Uses: Seeds are roasted and given to suck that gives relief in cough and smooths soar throat.

Zingiber officinale Rose. F: Zingiberaceae

Vernacular Names: E: Ginger; H: Adrak; B: Ada; M, S: Adhe; N: Adi.

Habit and Stature: It is a perennial creeping herb which is stout, horizontal, has tuberous rhizomes and is generally cultivated. It has antioxidant properties.

Parts Used: Rhizomes

Ethnomedicinal Uses: Rhizome is roughly crushed and fried in slow fire with pure ghee, and little sugar or *mishree* may be added to it. This sweet candy is given to suck slowly, but it is never chewed. It is good for dry cough and soothes sore throat.

Oil treatment

- A handful of pure mustard *Raphanus sativus* L. oil is put on the centre part of the head without warming it for getting relief from blocked nose and throat due to cold and cough.
- Five or seven podes of garlic are fried in a cup of mustard *Raphanus sativus* L. oil and preserved in a metal bowl. The bowl is put on slow fire every time before use and slightly heated. This lukeworm oil is massaged especially on the nails of fingers and toes.

FEVER

Nyctanthes arbortristis L. F: Oleaceae

Vernacular Names: E: Night jasmine, weeping nyctanthes; H: Harsingar; M: Saparom; S: Saparom; N: Murjhatni.

Habit and Stature: It is a small tree that commonly grows in the hills and rocky ravines. This tree has fragrant, white flowers with orange tubes that open in the evening and drop next morning. The corolla tubes yield an orange dye.

Parts Used: Leaves

Ethnomedicinal Uses: The decoction of fresh leaves is given twice daily for fever.

Crotalaria albida Heyne & Roth. F: Papilionaceae

Vernacular Names: M: Piri sokae, Bir Jhinri.

Habit and Stature: This herb or undershrub is one of the most common forest crotalarians that grows in abundance on hard clay soil of the hilly ground and it stems up to 3 ft high from a woody rootstock.

Parts Used: Root or whole plant

Ethnomedicinal Uses: The decoction of the herb or root is given twice, especially for fever in children.

Andrographis paniculata Nees. F: Acanthaceae

Vernacular Names: E: The creat, King of bitters; H: Kiryat, çhiretta; B: Kalmegh; Chiretta; M., Chiretta; S. Chiretta; Ku: Chiretta, N: Chiretta.

Habit and Stature: It is an erect branched annual herb which is 1ft to 3 ft high and is commonly found in the villages and forests.

Parts Used: Leaves, dry twigs

Ethnomedicinal Uses: Decoction of the fresh leaves or water of the dried twigs soaked in water overnight and is given in the morning and evening for curing malarial fever.

Azadirachta indica Juss. F: Meliaceae

Vernacular Names: E: The neem tree, the margosa tree; H, B: Neem; M: Nim daru; S: Nim dare; Ku, N: Nim.

Habit and Stature: It is a common tree that is usually planted but is also found in forest. It is a good venue tree that frequently grows on its own near gardens and villages. All parts of the tree are of various uses. The seed is collected for its oil which is used especially in parasitic skin diseases and for dressing foul ulcers. It is an anthelmintic and astringent.

Parts Used: Bark, leaves

Ethnomedicinal Uses: Decoction of bark or leaves is given twice daily in intermittent fever and malaria.

DIARRHOEA AND DYSENTERY

Ficus infectoria Roxb. F: Moraceae

Vernacular Names: H: Pilkan, Pakar; B: Pakar; M: Jojo hesa, Pepe hesa; S: Pakare; Ku: Kuajari; N: Putkal.

Habit and Stature: In all the districts of Chotanagpur, this medium or large sized tree grows that bears leaf buds which are usually pubescent flushed with whitish, red basal bracts.

Parts Used: Dried Leaf buds

Ethnomedicinal Uses: The fresh leaves buds on the onset of season is parboiled, dried, and stored. In case of diarrhoea and dysentery the dry leaf buds are boiled and this sour water is taken two to three times or according to the need.

Holarrhena antidysenterica Wall. F: Apocynacee

Vernacular Names: H, B: Koraiya, Kurchi; M: Toa baha; S: Haṭ baha; Ku: Korkora.

Habit and Stature: It is a large shrub or a small tree that is very common in the area and frequently grows on the laterite soil. The shrub has sweet scented, white flowers and hence the Mundari name, Toa baha i.e. flower like milk.

Parts Used: Bark, Seeds

Ethnomedicinal Uses: Powder of the bark of stem or root is given with water twice a day. Seeds are also excellent cure for the disease.

Shorea robusta Gaertn. F: Dipterocarpaceae

Vernacular Names: E: Sal tree; H, B: Sal; M: Sarjom daru; S: Sarjom dare; Ku: Makka; N: Sakhua.

Habit and Stature: This tree grows naturally throughout the area and attains 150 ft. height and 12 ft. girth but on the hills it is often small in size. The tree is worshipped and is of religious and socio-cultural importance in Jharkhand.

Parts Used: Bark, fruits, seeds

Ethnomedicinal Uses: Powder of the bark or decoction of the bark is given twice a day or as required. The fruit or seeds are boiled and eaten with salt as required.

DENTAL CARE

Clerodendrum infortunatum Gaertn: Verbenaceae

Vernacular Names: H: Bhant; B: Bhat; M: Chamgar, Kula marsal; S: Baṛni

Habit and Stature: A robust shrub or undershrub which commonly grows along streams and in shady places and edges of glades in the forest.

Parts Used: Tender stems

Ethnomedicinal Uses: Tender stem is used as toothbrush for strong teeth and dental problems.

Cuscuta reflexa Roxb. F: Cuscutaceae

Vernacular Names: E: Dodder; H: Amarbel; B: Algusi; M: Ará roanr; S: Alakjaṛi; Ku: Xorxo banda; N: banda.

Habit and Stature: It is a leafless, rootless parasite with thread like twinning stem that draws its food from the host with the help of suckers which penetrate deep into the tissues of the host.

Parts Used: The twinner

Ethnomedicinal Uses: The twinner is boiled in water and then cooled in normal temperature. This water is used as mouth wash and is used for pain in the teeth and gums.

Elephantopus scaber L. F: Asteraceae

Vernacular Names: H: Gobhi, Samdulan; M: Maráchuta; S: Mańjur jhuṭi; Ku: Minjur chundi; N: Jurbia.

Habit and Stature: An erect rigid herb that grows commonly in open ground and under partial shade in the forest.

Parts Used: Leaves

Ethnomedicinal Uses: Sap of the leaves is applied in the gums of children for easy teething.

Madhuca indica Gmel. F: Sapotaceae

Vernacular Names: E: Indian butter tree, Mahwah tree; H: Mahua; B: Maua, Mahua; M: Madukam; S: Matkom; Ku: Madgi; N: Mahua.

Habit and Stature: A large or medium sized tree with dense rounded rather low crown, pubescent or tomentose twigs that commonly grows in the forests. The tree demands light but likes a little shade when young. It is a very slow growing species. The seed yields oil which is edible. The oil cake has insecticidal properties.

Parts Used: Bark

Ethnomedicinal Uses: Bark is boiled extensively in water which is cooled at normal temperature and is used as mouthwash that tightens the loose teeth and cures the gums.

ECZYMA

Azadirachta indica Juss. F: Meliaceae

Vernacular Names: E: The neem tree, the margosa tree; H, B: Nim; M: Nim daru; S: Nim dare; Ku, N: Nim

Habit and Stature: It is a common tree that is usually planted but is also found in forest. It is a good venue tree that frequently grows on its own, near gardens and villages. All parts of the tree are of various uses. The seed is collected for its oil which is used especially in parasitic skin diseases and for dressing foul ulcers. It is an anthelmintic.

Parts Used: Leaves, Oil of the seed

Ethnomedicinal Uses: Paste of the fresh leaves or oil of the seed is applied many times in the affected area. Oil is put in the affected area with the feather of hen or birds.

Cassia tora L. F: Caesalpinaceae

Vernacular Names: H.B.: Chakund; M: Huring chakonda ará; S: Chakaonda; Ku: Sani chakonda; N: chakor.

Habit and Stature: It in an erect herb which is 1 inch to 5 inch in height. This herb is very common and sub gregarious which grows in waste ground and forest glades during the rainy season.

Parts Used: Leaves

Ethnomedicinal Uses: Leaves or seeds paste is applied in the affected part.

Chlorodendrum infortunatum Gaertn. F: Verbenaceae

Vernacular Names: H: Bhant; B: Bhat; M: Chamgar, Kula marsal; S: *Bạrni.*

Habit and Stature: A robust shrub or undershrub which commonly grows along streams and in shady places and edges of glades in the forest.

Parts Used: Leaves

Ethnomedicinal Uses: Leaves are boiled and this water is applied in the affected part many times.

Pongamia pinñata L. F: Papilionaceae

Vernacular Names: E: Indian beech; H: Karanj; M: Koronjo; S: Kuronj; Ku: Koronjo; N: Karanj.

Habit and Stature: It is a moderate or large tree that grows indigenously throughout the area along streams and forests. Though this tree growes naturally, it is also largely planted. The pods are collected for the valuable oil extracted from the seed which is used for burning and for the cure of skin diseases. It is a wonderful tree that can adapt itself to diverse conditions and is excellent for road side plantation. Possesses insecticidal and antibacterial properties.

Parts Used: Seed oil

Ethnomedicinal Uses: Oil of the seed is applied regularly in the affected part.

Sida cordifolia Burm. F: Malvaceae

Vernacular Names: E: Country mallow; H: Bariar; B: Bala; M: Marang lupu ará; S: Latha chipchirp.

Habit and Stature: It is an erect undershrub that is 2 ft to 4 ft. high and grows in wet places throughout the area, especially in scrub jungles.

Parts Used: Leaves

Ethnomedicinal Uses: Leaves paste is applied in the affected part.

GASTRO INTESTINAL AILMENTS

Aegle marmelos Correa. F: Rutaceae

Vernacular Names: E: The bael tree, wood apple; H: Bel; M:

Sidaru; S: Sińjạ dare, Ku: Xotta; N: Bel.

Habit and Stature: The tree is deciduous, aromatic and frost hardy but slow growing and it is moderate in size with one or two strong thorns from the leaf axils. It grows naturally on the hills and scrub jungles, but it is also planted. Ripe fruits have cooling, laxative, and nutritive properties. The rind of unripe fruit yields an orange dye.

Parts Used: Fruits

Ethnomedicinal Uses: The ripe fruit's pulp is mixed with water and little sugar (optional) and given in constipation and gastristis. Sometimes, the ripe pulp is only taken.

Centella asiatica L. F: Apiaceae

Vernacular Names: E: Indian pennywort; H: Mandukparni; B: Thol-Khuri; M: Choke ará; Ku: Muxa arxá; N: Beng sag.

Habit and Stature: It is a variable herb with long creeping stems, rooting at the nodes, young leaves and petioles villous. This herb is found more frequently in Chotanagpur and Singhbhum and grows mainly in wet places and fields. It is used greatly as pot herb and as remedy for many diseases. Women often dry and store it to use in summer (refer chapter I – Jogao Joton).

Parts Used: Whole plant

Ethnomedicinal Uses: It is consumed as dry powder with water once in morning for curing gastritis. To avoid its bitterness fresh or dry leaves are mixed with tomato and eaten as chutney with food for gastritis. It is also a common recipe for summer as it also has a cooling effect for stomach.

Polygala chinensis L. F: Polygalaceae

Vernacular Names: H: Madan mastak, Ratan purus; S: Tanr but.

Habit and Stature: It is an annual herb that mostly diffuse or decumbent and usually grows in grass lands, road sides, and fields.

Parts Used: Whole plant

Ethnomedicinal Uses: Plant paste with water or decoction of the whole plant is given to cure stomach ache.

Terminalia bellerica Gaertn. F: Combretaceae

Vernacular Names: E: Beleric myrabolan; H: Behra; B: Bohera; M: Lupung; S: Lopoṅg; Ku: Bahera; N: Bahra.

Habit and Stature: It is a large tree with straight and tall trunk that grows throughout the whole area, general in Sal forest and nearly always in valleys. It is used as medicine and is one of the constituents of Ayurvedic medicine "*triphala*".

Parts Used: Fruits

Ethnomedicinal Uses: Fruit powder is taken with water twice for curing stomach ache and indigestion.

Terminalia chebula Retz. F: Combretaceae

Vernacular Names: E: Chebulic myrabolan; H: Harra; B: Haritaki; M: Rola; S: Ro̲l; Ku: Harda, Hrra.

Habit and Stature: It is a moderate sized tree that grows throughout the area, commonly on the low hills and plateau. It is frost hardy and coppices well. The tree is greatly used in native medicines and is one of the constituents of Ayurvedic medicine "triphala".

Parts Used: Fruits

Ethnomedicinal Uses: Fruit powder is given twice daily for curing indigestion and gastristis.

POST-NATAL CARE

After childbirth due to weakness, infection, cold, etc., women suffer from fever, body pain etc. It is commonly known as "*parsauti*". *Baidhayas* or herbal practitioner gives specialized treatment, but lay women also know some remedies.

Terminalia arjuna Roxb. F: Combretaceae

Vernacular Names: E: Arjuna myrabolan; H: Arjun, Kahu; B: Arjun; M: Gara hanta; S: Kạhuạ.

Habit and Stature: A large tree commonly grows along *nalas* where it sometimes attains great size. It chiefly occupies the valleys of the dryer hilly districts and is not very common in Santhal Pargana. It is naturally cultivated along road side for afforestation programmes. The bark is used in native medicine as a tonic, astringent and is said to be useful in heart diseases and ulcers.

Parts Used: Bark

Ethnomedicinal Uses: Decoction of bark given is used for *parsauti* (Perpurial fever) twice daily.

Terminalia bellerica Gaertn. F: Combretaceae

Vernacular Names: E: Beleric myrabolan; H: Behra; B: Bohera; M: Lupung; S: Lopoṅg; Ku: Bahera; N: Bahra.

Habit and Stature: It is a large tree with straight and tall trunk that grows throughout the whole area, generally in *Sal* forest and nearly always in valleys. It is used as medicine and is one of the constituents of Ayurvedic medicine "triphala".

Parts Used: Bark

Ethnomedicinal Uses: Decoction of the bark about four tablespoon twice daily for one week or fifteen days is given in post-natal care.

Ludwigia perennis L. F: Onagraceae

Vernacular Names: M: Gara sigigit, Sukuri pota; S: Parsauti ghas.

Habit and Stature: A herb of 8" to 18" high and is usually erect and glabrous that is commonly growns in the rice fields and wet places.

Parts Used: Whole plant

Ethnomedicinal Uses: Decoction of the plant is given in *parsauti* (Perpurial fever). The Santhali name is most relevant for the disease.

Celastrus paniculata Wild. F: Celastraceae

Vernacular Names: E: Climbing Staff; H.B.: Malkangni; M.S. Kujri; Ku: Kujur.

Habit and Stature: It is a woody liana growing throughout the region and is a deciduous climbing shrub that has rough pale brown exfoliating bark, covered densely with small elongated lenticles.

Parts Used: Seed Oil.

Ethnomedicinal Uses: One teaspoon of oil of the seed is given after childbirth for one week or fifteen days, and is said to cure infection, weakness etc.

SUN STROKE

Allium cepa L. F: Liliaceae

Vernacular Names: E: Onion; H: Piaz; B: Piyaj; M, Ku, S, N: Peaj.

Habit and Stature: It is a perennial herb that is largely cultivated. The bulb and leaves are used commonly in Indian kitchen as vegetable for flavouring and pickling. It is stimulant, diuretic, and expectorant. The fresh juice contains bactericidal properties.

Parts Used: Bulb

Ethnomedicinal Uses

- During hard summer months one onion bulb preferably the white variety is put inside the cloth wear in such a way that it touches the body. It is said to be a prevention from sun stroke.
- Raw peace of onion bulb is eaten with rice mixed with water (*Pani bhat*). It is supposed to give a cooling effect to the body.
- Raw bulb is grinded, and the paste is applied on the body especially in the sole and palms of the victim of sun stroke.

Mangifera indica L. F: Anacardiaceae

Vernacular Names: E: Mango; H: Aam; M: Uli; Ku; Tatkha; N: Aam.

Habit and Stature: The tree is found in the wild as well as is cultivated. It has been introduced in other warm regions of the world. The species appears to have been domesticated. It is the largest fruit tree with 30 ft to 100 ft height and a broad rounded canopy.

Parts Used: Fruit

Ethnomedicinal Uses

- Green mango is roasted or boiled. The pulp is rubbed in the body especially in the palms and sole of the victim.
- Green mango *Mangifera indica* L. is roasted or boiled and is mixed in water with sugar and little bit of salt. This *sharbat* (sweet drink) is taken as a preventive for sun stroke.

HEADACHE

Cassia fistula L. F: Caesalpiniaceae

Vernacular Names: E: The Indian laburunum, Purging cassia; H: Amaltas, Sonali; B: Bandar lathi; M: Hari, Bandar lauri; S: Ńuṛuć; Ku: Sonaraki.

Habit and Stature: A small or medium sized tree that has very beautiful bright yellow flowers in pendulous raceme. It grows throughout the area naturally or is planted. It is indifferent to soil and aspect but never at all gregarious. The tree frequently grows on the laterite soil and coppices readily.

Parts Used: Leaves

Ethnomedicinal Uses: Paste of fresh leaves is put on the forehead.

Vitex negundo L. F: Verbenaceae

Vernacular Names: E: Chaste tree, five leaved chaste tree; M: Bigna, Huhuri, sursing; S: Sinduạri; Ku: Xonxor; N: Sinduar.

Habit and Stature: A large strongly scented shrub that grows frequently in waste ground and hedges in the whole area. It is usually found near the villages and sometimes near river banks and is used in native medicine.

Parts Used: Leaves

Ethnomedicinal Uses: Leaves are grinded with onion bulb (white variety) and mixed with mustard oil and put on the forehead.

Anisomeles indica ktze. F: Lamiaceae

Vernacular Names: E: Indian catmint; H: Kalabhangra; M: Sega chálam, Marang sukuripota; S. Bharni; Ku, N: Mahadeo jata.

Habit and Stature: A strong smelling softly pubescent herb that is common in Santhal Paragana, and is frequent in Chotanagpur region, mainly found in the dry deciduous forests and wasteland. It is an aromatic plant with various medicinal uses. It has carminative, astringent and tonic properties.

Parts Used: Root

Ethnomedicinal Uses: Root paste is applied on the forehead.

CRMY (INTESTINAL PINWORMS)

Oryza sativa L. F: Poaceae

Vernacular Names: E: Rice, H: Chawal; B: Chal; M: Chauli; S: Cawle; Ku: Tikhil.

Habit and Stature: It is annual grass with creeping or floating and erect stems that is cultivated in the areas which are irrigated or submerged during rains as well as on non-submerged land. Different varieties but at present genetically modified varities are the available staple food of Jharkhand.

Parts Used: Rice seed

Ethnomedicinal Uses: *Usna* (boiled variety) rice is roasted till black. It is given to children to eat whenever they like. It is supposed that worms will come out, and hence a popular method for extraction of worms in case of small children.

Cyperus rotundus L. F: Cyperaceae

Vernacular Names: E: Nut grass; H: Nager motha; B: Moothoo, Mutha, Naragimothee; M: Piri Jimtu; S: Muthạ ghãs; Ku: Motha ghasi; N: Motha ghas.

Habit and Stature: A small, slendar sedge, commonly a weed, that is found all over the area. The whole plant is glabrous and somewhat glaucous. The tubers have a pleasant fragrance and are about 0.5" in diameter, which are ovoid, black or dark brown outside, and is white from inside.

Parts Used: Tubers

Ethnomedicinal Uses: The tubers are given to eat.

Adina cordifolia Hook. F: Rubiaceae

Vernacular Names: H: Karam; M: Kumba, Kurumba; S: Kurum;

Ku: Karam; N: Karam.

Habit and Stature: A large tree that grows naturally throughout the area. The tree is of religious and socio-cultural importance in Jharkhand.

Parts Used: Leaves

Ethnomedicinal Uses: Juice extract of fresh leaves is taken as required.

JAUNDICE

Aegle marmelos Correa. F: Rutaceae

Vernacular Names:: E: The bael tree, wood apple; H: Bel; M: Sinju daru; S: Sinjạ dare, Ku: Xotta; N: Bel.

Habit and Stature: The tree is deciduous, aromatic and frost hardy but slow growing and it is moderate in size with one or two strong thorns from the leaf axils. It grows naturally on the hills and scrub jungles, but it is also planted. Ripe fruits have cooling, laxative, and nutritive properties.

Parts Used: Leaves

Ethnomedicinal Uses: One leaf is grinded with three peppers and given thrice daily for seven days.

Centella asiatica L. F: Apiaceae

Vernacular Names: E: Indian pennywort; H: Mandukparni; B: Thol-Khuri; M: Choke ará; Ku: Muxa arxá; N: Beng sag.

Habit and Stature: It is a variable herb with long creeping stems, rooting at the nodes, young leaves and petioles villous. This herb is found more frequently in Chotanagpur and Singhbhum and grows mainly in wet places and fields. It is used greatly as pot herb and as remedy for many diseases. Women often dry and store it to use in summer (refer chapter I – Jogao Joton).

Parts Used: Whole plant

Ethnomedicinal Uses: Extract of the grinded fresh plant, mixed with *mishree* about four tablespoons for adults or four teaspoons for children is given in the morning when their stomach is empty till the symptom persists.

Phyllanthus niruri L. F: Euphorbiaceae

Vernacular Names: H: Jar amla, Bhuin amla; B: Bhuin amla; M: Muikoa Kantar, ote meral; S: ṭaṇḍimeral; Ku: Bhuin aunra; N: Jaramla.

Habit and Stature: It is an erect, very slender, and glabrous annual herb that is commonly a weed that grows probably all over the area. Fruits are small, globose, and form a row on the underside of the branchlets. The plant is considered as deobstrudent, diuretic, astringent, and for cooling body. It is applied in case of jaundice, dropsy, and genito-urinary infections.

Parts Used: Whole plant

Ethnomedicinal Uses: The extract of the grinded plant is mixed with *mishree* and is given in the morning when their stomach is empty till symptom persists.

Ricinus communis L. F: Euphorbiaceae

Vernacular Names: E: Castor oil plant; H: Erand; B: Aranda; M: Bindi, Ranga bindi; S: eraḍom; Ku: Digherendi; N: Erandi.

Habit and Stature: A stout wild shrub, often cultivated for its seeds which are rich in oil. The castor oil has more than 250 uses and is presently an important vegetable oil for industrial purposes. It is cathartic and mild laxative and is used as lubricant. The oil cake is used as manure. The stem yields paper pulp.

Parts Used: Leaves

Ethnomedicinal Uses: Juice extracted from fresh leaves is mixed with equal amount of coconut milk and is taken for three days or till the symptom persists.

Notes

1. *Adivashi Aushad (Horopathy)*, P.P. Hembrom.
2. *Mundari Dictionary*, Dr. M. M. Mundu, p. 783.
3. *Ibid.*, p. 757.
4. *Ibid.*, p. 98.

3

Forest Flora

Signature of Culture of Jharkhand

Culture of any traditional society is based on many factors such as topography, climate, ecology, biodiversity, etc. One of the major measures related to the culture of a region is based on the vegetational resource management of the particular place. Habit, human and habitat admix together develop a particular behavioural pattern of that region. Every habit of the residing community is correlated with the biological resources around it, be it clothing, eating, hunting, fishing, housemaking, etc. In the evolutionary steps to civilization, vegetation co-existed along with human being and *vice versa*.

The traditional culture of the tribes of Jharkhand has been structuralized in the same way for thousands of years. Tribes are the sons of the soil and live intermingled with nature and are nurtured by natural ecosystem. Forest plays a quintessential role in their living pattern. Existence of their everyday life is based on plants that grow around them which is adapted in the living attaire, totems, taboos, economic, religious and social ethos. Since ages some plants have made their vital presence in such a way that its importance in the community life cannot be ignored. From birth to death, in every sphere of life, these plants play a major role. From generation to generation, utilization of these plants has been accepted. With the passing years, time and test and long time usage has made indelible imprints as the culture of Jharkhand.

Uses of some plant species and ultimately their conversion as signature of culture of Jharkhand has been described below: Some culturally and traditionally linked forest species are:

SIGNIFICANCE AND USES OF PARTS OF *SAL* TREE

Shorea robusta Gaertn.

Family: Dipterocarpaceae

Vernacular name: E: The Sal tree; H, B: Sal; M, S, Ho: Sarjom; Ku: Makka; N: Sakhua.

Sal tree is the dominant species in the forests of Jharkhand. The tree holds a key position and is a vital component in the life of tribals. A Sal forest stands as a father figure fulfilling their daily needs. Their religious, economic, cultural and social life is mingled with this tree. It is a pillar of sustenance and every part of the tree is useful for the tribes. Throughout the year leaves and twigs are gathered from the tree. During summer, fruits and seeds are collected. It is the duty of the females to collect all the necessities in its due time.

The Leaves

A leaf of Sal is not just a green lamina; rather it is representative of the culture and tradition of Jharkhand. Leaves of the tree are used not just as a commodity; rather designing varied artefacts with leaves is an art in itself. Plucking of leaves from the forest, stiching to make various artefacts and selling it, is not only a manual work but is a symbol of peace and harmony, rhythm of affection and grace, mirror of hardship and duty, subject of poetry and songs (Ch. 4). It is unimaginable that a mere leaf has the capability of repleting human life in such a wonderful way.

heć sakam—*Plucking of Leaves—A Culture in Itself*

heć sakam is a *Mundari* name of an exclusive act of going to the forest to pluck leaves necessary for making leaf plates and cups required for a feast.

Plucking of green leaves usually of Sal is a salient feature of tribal life. It is mandatory for women to go to the forest to fetch leaves and make utility items from it. Plucking of leaves requires special skill, as only the mature healthy leaves with its pedicel are broken from the twig one by one. This requires skill as well as patience. Only a woman has the delicacy, daintiness, competence, and patience to perform this special task.

Utility Items and association with Culture

After the leaves are plucked they are stitched together with *chiri* (pins made of fine bamboo strips especially for stiching leaves) and utility items like leaf plates (*pattals*) and leaf cups (*donas*) are made to serve food. Sometimes *Khala*, that is, bigger leaf cup made to keep goodies in it is made. Various things are preserved in a scientific and healthy manner in *Sakam potom*, that is, special leaves ball made exclusively to preserve dry edibles (Ch. 1).

Sign of Social Harmony and Culture

In tribal villages of Jharkhand each and every small gesture reflects social harmony and distinct culture. It is observable in every occassion. During wedding or any other celebration in a house, the ladies of the village go to pluck leaves from the forest and in their leisure time (which is scanty looking at their busy schedule) gather in the concerned house and make leaf plates and cups. In a few days, ample of leaf plates and cups are ready for the feast, and the host does not have to worry or bear the burden of arranging or buying these things for the feast. A rich culture practised by simple people is exhibited in this ordinary task.

Economy and Culture

In the village markets, one can see that little amount of forest produces or small fishes are kept in a leaf and each leaf is sold for five, ten or fifteen rupees. A leaf with its commodites is called *kheza.* This is a unique method of measurement in tribal economy and culture since ancient time.

A Work of Art

The above described endeavour is not merely a regular manual task performed by tribal women but is a classic which has touched the sensitive heart of tribal poets and writers. It is described beautifully in folklores and songs in all tribal languages of Jharkhand (Ch. 4).

Way of Sustenence

The fresh green leaves are procured from the Sal tree by the women. They stitch these leaves with *chiri* (pins made exclusively by fine bamboo slits for stitching leaves) for making utility items such as leaf plates (*pattals*) and curry cups (*donas*). About a decade back, these leaf plates were used extensively in small functions at home, in marriage ceremonies and festivals to serve food. Large number of people even crowds were served food in the leaf plates.

When thermocol plates were not in the market, these leaf plates were in great demand. Tribal women were the regular suppliers of these plates and cups. They used to get orders in advance for making these plates and cups during marriage ceremonies, *puja utsav* etc. It used to be a good profitable business. Presently, the fresh leaf plates are modified by modern technology and pressed dry leaf plates are available in the market. It has been adopted and some women are also earning well from it.

The unique features of Sal leaf plates are the following:

- Environment friendly and biodegradable nature.
- Healthy way of eating as the leaf is thrown after use.
- Symbolizes religious, auspicious, special and joyous occasions.
- Pure Indian way of eating.
- **The Fruits** – The fruits of Sal are consumed as well as sold.
- **The Seeds** – *Sal* seeds are eaten when there is scarcity of rice, but it is unwholesome.
- **Oil** – Oil is extracted from the seeds and is used for cooking and burning.
- **Latex** – Latex known as *Sarjom lore* (M, S), that is, Tears of *Sal*. The Sal tree is tapped to get resin known as H: *dhuna*, M, S: *Sarjom lore*, Tears of Sal or latex. It is used in religious ceremonies and as air purifier. It is also used for medicinal purpose as well as for caulking by the villagers.
- **Bark** – Bark of Sal is employed as tan and is used as spices in the barbecue to the hunt by the tribal hunters.

- **The young shoots** – The young shoots are used as *datoon*, that is, tooth brush. It is used at home as well as sold from door to door and in the local market. Tribals especially women collect these twigs and sell it.

SIGNIFICANCE AND USES OF *PALAS* TREE

Butea monosperma Lamk

Family: Papilionaceae.

Vernacular name: H: Palas, Tesu, Dhak; B: Palas; M: Murud; S: Murup̓; Ku: Makka; N: Parsa.

- **The Green Leaves** – In the regions where Sal trees are scanty, the leaves of palas are used as alternative for making Leaf plates (*pattals*) and curry cups (*donas*). These are plucked and stitched by the women and sold in the village and local markets. It is also a source of women empowerment that is similar to that of making and selling utility items from the Sal leaves.
- **The Flowers** – The beautiful reddish orange coloured flowers of palas are used as dye.
- **The Seeds** – The seeds are used as medicine.

Significance and Uses of *Mahua* Tree

Madhuca Indica Gmel

Family: Sapotaceae.

Vernacular name: E: Indian butter tree; H, B, N: Mahua; M: Madkom; S: Makom Ku: Madgi.

Parts of *Mahua* Tree and Its Uses:

- **Flowers:** The flowers of Mahua are significant to the people of Jharkand. It may be called famine food. In the scarcity of rice, the flowers of Mahua are used as wholesome food. The dried flowers are sold in the market. Country liquor is made from it. Onset of summer brings the sweet scented yellowish cream Mahua flowers that are collected mostly by women and children on the wee hours of morning.

- **Fruits:** The fruits of Mahua is called B: *Kochra*, S: *Bakṛi*, M: *Pako*. The young fruits are cooked as vegetable. The dried ones are used at home as well as sold in the market.
- **Seed:** The kernel of Mahua is called B: *Kuindi*, S: *kũinḍi*, M: *dola*. Oil is extracted from the Mahua seeds known as *kuindi sunum* which are used for various purpose, for preparing curry, for anointing, for lubricating cart wheels and as a medicine also.
- **Twigs:** Tender twigs are used as tooth brush.
- **Bark:** Bark is said to be a cure for gum diseases.
- **Cake (S: *kũinḍi*):** Oil Cake (S: kaṛe) left after the oil from the seed has been extracted is used in case of indigestion. It is used as fish poison and as snake replicant (it is burnt and the smoke drives the snake away).
- ***Mahua laṭhae̱*: special tribal food:** Mahua ***laṭhae̱*** is a special tribal food prepared from dry "Mahua"—*Madhuca indica* Gmel—flowers. The food may also be called famine food as it is used during adverse time.

The main crop of Jharkhand is the paddy crop. The farmers depend on the monsoon, but mostly the yield is poor and lasts only for six months. During the next monsoon, the farmers take out the rice seeds (*dhan*) that are kept reserved for paddy cropping, and thereafter little or no grain left at home to eat. At this time of adversity, the dried Mahua flowers comes handy. The lady of the house has already collected, dried and kept these flowers safely during summer itself. Now she takes out these dried flowers for special processing. These dry flowers are boiled in slow fire. Dry *Sal—Shorea robusta* Gaertn—fruits or Cotyledons of "Tamarind"—*Tamarindus indica L.*—or Seeds of 'Arhar'—*Cajanus cajan* L.—Or "Kulthi'—*Dolichos biflorus* L.—or 'Sem'—*dichos lablab* L.—can also be mixed in the boiling flowers. It may be called a poor man's sweet dish, but it is tasty, wholesome and proved to be very nutritive.

Significance and Uses of Puff Balls and Mushrooms

Lycoperdon Sp.

Class: Lycoperdaceae.
Vernacular name: E: Puff ball, N: Rugra, M: Putu, S: Putkạ, Ku: Putu.

Agaricus Sp.

Class: Agaricaceae

Vernacular name: E: Mushroom, H: Kukurmuta, S: Ot́; M: Ud, N: Khukri, Ku: Osa. *Lycoperdon* and *Agricus* species are the gift of nature to the tribal people. These grow abundantly in the Sal forest during the rainy season. The edible species are well recognized by the tribals and are considered great delicacy and its collection is a pleasure for children and women. These are cooked at home and also sold in the market. Now-a-days it fetches quite a good amount.

Significance and Uses of Bamboo

Bambusa Sp.

Family: Poaceace.

Vernacular name: E: Bamboo; H, N: Bans; M: Mad′; S: Mat́; Ku: Katanga; B: Ketua.

Parts Used:

- **Bamboo shoots:** New tender bamboo shoots are known as *karils*. During rainy season, new bamboo shoots come out in the old bamboo groves. These young and tender shoots are known as H: *Karil*, M: *Helta*. These young shoots are cut finely and used at home as vegetable, curry and pickle. These are also sold in the market.
- ***"Sandhana"* the great bamboo pickle:** Bamboo pickle

called *'Sandhana'* is famous in Jharkhand. The new tender *karils* are cut finely and processed through indigenous method. These are wrapped in 'gungu patta'—*Bauhinia variegata* L.—leaves to maintain its freshness and taste. Tribal women earn a good sum in the season by selling *Sandhana* in the market. Its quality is judged by its fine texture and taste. The water in it is evaporated and pickle is prepared at home. This unique tribal pickle is so popular that the tribals residing out of Jharkhand make it sure to get this pickle in time through friends and relatives. Sandhana is the identity of Jharkhand as well as means of sustainability. The tribal women and their family get benefited from it.

- ***Hạnḍuạ:*** The young and tender bamboo shoots, that is, *karils* are cut finely, sundried and coarsely pounded. This coarse powder is called ***Hạnḍuạ***. These are stored safely for occasional use. ***Hạnḍuạ*** is also sold in the market. *Chatni* is prepared from it. It is also mixed in fish curry especially of small fishes like Gatoo, Bumbui, etc. The preparation is also considered a great delicacy.
- **Articles of Bamboo:** Many articles for domestic usage are made from the bamboo stems. The cut bamboo strips are made into different things like *Soop*, *Daura*, *Tappa*, *Chata*, *Kumni* (Fish trap), *Jharoo* (Broom), etc. These items are used extensively in the villages of Jharkhand, hence, these are in great demand in the local market.

Significance and Uses of Palm (*Khajur*) Tree:

Phoenix Sylvestris Roxb.

Family: Arecaceae

Vernacular name: H: Khajur, N: Khijur, Ku: Khijri, M: Kita; S: Khijur

Labour Not in Vain

An old tribal woman—who has no strength to go to the forest and fields for hard manual work because of her old age—does not sit ideally and waste her time in vain. She keeps herself busy in more constructive work. The old tribal woman sitting at home makes many articals from *Khijur* leaves. She weaves plates of *Khijur* leaves, stitches it and makes *paṭiạ* (Mats). These are used at home to sit and sleep in it. The young ladies may help her in their leisure time. The *paṭiạ* is are in great demand in villages and are regularly sold in the village markets. Thus, the *Khijur* leaves are a financial aid to the tribal women especially the old ones. It keeps the old grandma busy and gives financial aid to her.

The Unique Feature of **Khijur** *paṭiạ*

- It symbolizes culture and rich heritage of Jharkhand.
- Spreading of the *paṭiạ* and offering to sit on it is considered a sign of welcome and honour to a guest.
- In all the auspicious occasions like *Lotapani* (engagement ceremony), *Biha* (marriage ceremony), etc., bride and bridegroom are asked to stand or sit in a brand new *Khijur paṭiạ*.
- It is a sentimental gift and fond remembrance for a daughter or younger generation from an old mother or grandmother.
- These mats are biodegradable and eco-friendly.
- It symbolises the scientific approach of tribals towards living life. The specialty of *paṭiạ* is that it is cool in summer but is warm in the cold winter months. Thus, it is a relief for the poor.
- It symbolises the rentless labour and prestige of tribal women even in old age.
- It symbolises respect given to the dead, which is a special part of Jharkhand's culture because a dead body is wrapped in the *paṭiạ* for last cremation.

Plate 1: Collection of plant resources in wilderness

Plate 2: Broom making from grasses

Plate 3: Selling of pot herbs and leaves

Plate 4: Forest artifacts in the market

Plate 5: Collected mahua flowers

Plate 6: Girls collecting forest goods in group

Plate 7: Wild mushrooms fetches good price

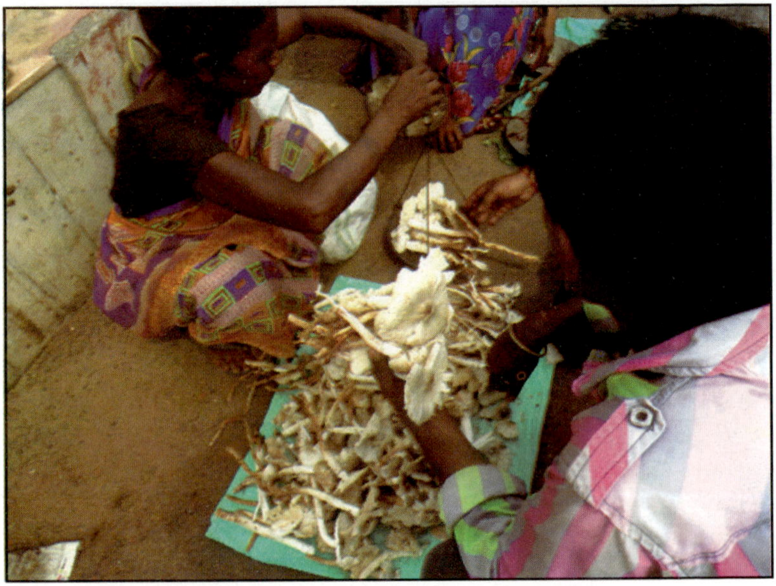

Plate 8: Busy in selling mushrooms - a forest product

Plate 9: Forest grasses and asset of economic

Plate 10: Selling sandhna - i.e. bamboo shoots

Plate 11: Fuel woods from forest

Plate 12: Collection of forest commodities

Plate 13: Goods from bamboo

Plate 14: Stitching of sal leaf plates

Plate 15: Fruits, dried and fresh forest product - means of sustenance

Plate 16: A forest species

Plate 17: *Gunj Abrus* precatorius (a medicinal plant)

4
Connected Folklores

Folklores are the reflection of human life. Human life holds many phases of journey in itself. Every human being has their own journey of life. Every step of life has its own colour—from the careless childhood to the fragrent youth as well as from dutiful adulthood and wise old age.

Folklores are written in the background of village life. Every phase of village life is observed by the poets and authors who have lived that life and have experienced its rich colours. They have earnestly penned it down and have given their immortal contribution to the society in terms of folklores.

Folklores can never be artificial, as they come from the natural rhythm of life. It is spontaneous, simple, and natural. Experience of life comes out through words and form of songs. It is never an outcome of a serious reading or intellectual thinking; rather it is a discource about common people's life in simple words which contains profound meaning. Words for folklore come out spontaneously by gazing at the cosmic world and flora and fauna around us. The physical activity and experience of social environment takes the shape of folk songs.

Here, we have chosen some precious souvenir from the valuable collection of folklores, which describe the plant-human relationship. It describes the landscape, climate and related habit of the natural flora. The availability of local flora on the hills, forests, bank of rivers, marshy land in related months and season are described so well that going through the lines a picturesque description appears vividly before the eyes. The songs impart physiological knowledge of flowering, fruiting, opening of buds, and abscission of leaves in its due time. In the folklores, some species of the floral world have been described repeatedly in all the tribal languages. It must be due to its immense relationship with human being. These species are common in the natural forests and are closely embedded in the socio-cultural life of the people. The description of Sal—*Shorea robusta* Gaertn—tree comes often in all tribal languages. It is because of its importance in the economic, religious, socio-cultural characteristics of the region. Another tree species is Mahua—*Madhuca indica* Gmel—which is also frequently described in the songs because of its beauty and various utility. There are many other species which are close to the heart of native people and often described in the folklores.

The folklore expresses the significance of forest in a native life. The types of vegetation, its habit and habitation, the geography of the land, the climate, every part is connected with the ethnic life. Their life without the natural biota is unimaginable.

The utmost importance of the chosen folklores is the depiction of the intrinsic relationship a tribal woman experiences with nature. It explains her portrayal as a female who looks for support and sustenance to the forest and expresses her joy when she goes to gather the flowers and fruits. Furthermore, the folklore describes the pleasure she experiences while plucking wild flowers to adorn herself along with her hurriedness to pick green leaves in its due time. It also demonstrates her agony while climbing rocky hills and crossing thorn bushes in addition to her obedience for the taboos and norms the society has set for her. Going through all these phases of life; her joy, sorrow, pleasure, agony, and responsibility come to her lips in the form of sweet melodies.

The poets have captured her every mood in their songs and poems. The beautiful lyrics are written in various tribal languages of Jharkhand, that is, in Mundari, Santhali, Kharia, Ho and Kurukh. Going through the lines is a pleasure for the reader as it portrays a glimpse of forests of Jharkhand vibrant with the picture of tribal woman. Her hard work, her strength and delicacy truly proves the Munda phrase which quotes:

> ***Kaji ge during***
> ***Senge susun***
>
> to speak is to sing
> to walk is to dance

Santhali Folklores

1.

Burre Sarjom baha
lodopé – lodopé Sarjom baha
Birre Murut' baha
Beńged –jeńget' Murut' baha

[*Sarjom* flowers in the forest
Swinging, dangling, Sarjom flowers
Murut' flowers in the forest
Shining shimmering, *Murut'* flowers]

The poet is enchanted by the beauty of the forest. He states that *Sarjom* flowers are blooming in the forest and bunches of flowers are swinging softly in the air. *Murut'* flowers are also in full bloom and are shining and gleaming in at the same time.

Sal ("*Sarjom*" *Shorea robusta* Gaertn) is the dominant species of the natural forests of Jharkhand. The flowers are pale white or creamy and bloosoms in bunches. On the onset of flowering season, fragnance of the flowers fills the whole forest.

Palas ("*Murut'* " *Butea monosperma* Lamk) is the state flower of Jharkhand and blosoms during spring. The flowers have vivid reddish orange colour and so these flowers are perfectly named as "flame of the forest". During spring (March – April), the whole forest becomes colourful because of the radience of the Palas flowers.

In the poetry, the lines present a vivid picture of the beauty of the forest.

2.

Sińbirre Sarjom sakam
Dela dai lań heć ạgui
Man birre Matkom sakam
Dela dại lań heć ạgui
[*Sarjom* leaves in the Siń forest
Let's go to pluck, O dai,
Matkom leaves in the Maan forest
Let's go to pluck, O dai.]

The song describes the eagerness of a young girl to work. She is telling her *dai* (elder sister) about the abundance of *Sarjom* and *Matkom* leaves in the *Siń* and *Maań* forest, respectively and is asking her dai to accompany her to the forest so that together they can pluck the leaves.

Sal ("*Sarjom*" *Shoera robusta* Gaertn) and Mahua ("*Matkom*" *Madhuca India* Gmel) are the two prominent tree species found in the forests of Jharkhand. *Sarjom* is a tree of multifarious use and so is *Matkom*.

The song makes the reader acquainted with the indigenous tradition of gathering forest produces, such as leaves, flowers, buds, young shoots, pot herbs, etc., and it is considered a feminine job—" *heć sakam*", that is, plucking of leaves is a specific work done only by females (Ch. III P). It is a daily task though labourious but often enjoyable also. Going to the forest means encountering the dangers of the wild. To safeguard the female, the society has made taboo that women cannot go to the forest alone but in groups at least of two (Ch. 1P). Therefore, in the song the girl is requesting her elder sister to come with her to the forest.

Siń[1] and *Maań*[2] forest are the places mentioned in formal talks, folklores and folk tales of the Santhals. It is said that in this forest Pilchu Haram (the first man) took his sons to hunt. *Maañ* forest is described in a Dasai song "the day Maan earth has become fine dust."

3.

Sid me se gateń ho,
Sarjom baha do
Tiog me se sańań ho,
Ńuṛukuć baha do
Sut're iń bahaea,
Ńuṛukuć baha do

[Just pluck, O friend
Sarjom flowers
Just pluck, O friend,
Ńuṛukuć flowers
I will adorn my hair, O friend
with *Ńuṛukuć* flower]

The song expresses the desire of a girl to ornate herself with the flowers of the forest. She is asking her friend to pluck *Sarjom* and *Ńuṛukuč* flowers which she will put in her hair to adorn herself.

Here the floral biodiversity of the natural forests of Santhal Pargana is articulated. Sal ("Sarjom" *Shorea robusta* Gaertn v. n.: H) has beautiful cream coloured flowers that grow in bunches and these flowers have very sweet fragrance. It is the dream of every girl to decorate herself with Sarjom flowers. Amaltas ("Nurukuc" *Cassia fistula* L. v. n. H) has bright yellow showy pendulous flowers which is also a favourite of girls because with these flowers they adorn their hairs.

The aesthetic element present in the socio-cultural life of indigenous society is also suggested in this song. They do not ornate themselves with flowers which are cultivated but they prefer the forest species. Their religious rituals and culture is based on the flowers of the forest species.

4.

Teheń dole numakan Tuṛi pukhrire
Teheń dole naṛkawakan Baha bandelare
Gapa dole bohaea Sarjom baha
Gapa dole bahaea Miru baha

[Today, we have bathed in *Tuṛi pukhrire*,
Today, we have washed hair in *Baha bandelare*
Tomorrow, we will worship the *Sarjom* flowers
Tomorrow, I'll ornate with *Miru* flowers.]

This song describes the portrait of a girl who is preparing herself for the worship ceremony of a festival, most probably the "*Baha Parob*." The girl is telling that they (females) have taken bath in *Tuṛi pukhrire* and have cleaned their long tessel in *Baha bandelare*. The following day, they will worship the *Sarjom* flowers and for that occasion she will adorn her hair with *Miru* flowers.

Sal is a dominant forest species of great religious importance. The tree is worshiped in Jharkhand and many rituals are performed with its leaves and flowers. Great ecstacy prevails among people and lots of preparation takes place before the festivals. It is but natural for the girls to clean themselves and adorn their hairs with the forest flowers to look beautiful in any specific occasion.

"Miru baha" (*Abutilan indicum* Don. v. n. H: Kanhi) is a cream coloured flower. It is very well described in the Santhal folk songs and poems.

"*Naṛka*"[12] is a special method of washing hair among Santhals and other tribes of Jharkhand. They wash their hair with fine clay and not soap. The clay makes the hair clean, bouncy and shining more than any soap or shampoo.

"Tuṛi pukhrire" and "*Baha bandelare*"[13] are the names of water reservoirs of different sizes. *"Tuṛi pukhrire*" and "*Baha bandelare*" are always joined together. These are places mentioned in the tradition. The song symbolizes the rhythmic relation that exists between various decorative and ritualistic activities and puts forth the emotional lives of the tribal girl and woman.

5.

Nalope calak'
Siń birte do
Siń bir ko Sendraekań,
Nalope Calaḱ
Maań birte do
Maań bir ko karkaekan.

[Don't you go, to the *Siń* forest
Hunting is going on
Don't you go, to the *Maań* forest
Hunting is going on.]

The gentle protective tone of the song beautifully expresses the attitude towards young girls in the society. The composer of the song is warning young girls not to go to the *Siń* and *Maań* forest for carrying out their daily chores as hunting is going on there.

"Hunting" here means the traditional annual hunt done by the indigenous men. It is celebrated as an annual feast. In this day, all men gather in the morning with their traditional weapons. The traditional drums echo the village and the forest. Together a large number of men cover the forest, search, run and hunt for the whole day. In the evening, they celebrate and eat their cooked hunts. It is a dayout for men from their labourious task of agriculture and other routine works. It is a day of refreshing and rejoicing.

The normal work of women is to go to the forest for procuring forest products. On the particular day which is celebrated as the traditional annual hunt day, females are banned from visiting the forest. Accidents may happen and men will have difficulty in shooting and running after the prey. The agitated wild animal may attack the women.

The protective spirit of the song is collective. It spells the care with which women are treated by the community. The gentle overtone of care and respect for women pervades the entire spirit of their lives.

6.

Siń bir doń senoḱgea
Sakam heć lagit'
Paseć do gatetińe senakan
Maan bir doń dukangea
Sahan mag lạgit'
Paseć do sańańtińe senakana

[Yet, I will go to the *Siń* forest
to pluck leaves
May be my friend is there
I will go to the *Maań* forest
to cut woods
May be my friend is there.]

This poem interweaves the subtle romance in the heart of the youth. In spite of restriction, the girl is adamant to go to the *Siń* forest to pluck leaves. She wants to go to the *Maań* forest to cut woods. In her heart, she hopes her friend (it seems a male friend) will be in forest. She wants to meet him and is making excuses to continue her daily work in spite of forbidding.

Plucking leaves and cutting firewoods is the usual task of female. They go daily to the forest except the annual hunt day as on that particular day women are forbidden from going to the forest.

Siń forest and *Maań* forest are probably imaginary places that are described in the folktales and folklores of the Santhals.

The poem has a sophisticated structure of a love lyric. "Yet, I will go"—the refrain very quietly resonates the circumstances, the prohibitions against the meeting which may be for safety but it asserts the determination in the young heart. These small moments of desires strewn with care and anxiety bring out the sensitive and human aspects of the routine life of a tribal girl.

Mundari Folklores

1.
Toa Ba

Toa-ba-na dai
Toa-ba
Urae-barae dai
Atal ba.

Mogo-mogo-a
Toa-ba
Taral-taral
Atal-ba

Got' lea lang
Toa-ba
Totak' lea lang
Atal-ba

Sala-lea lang
Ala-ba
Gutu lea-lang
Mala-ba
Supit′-supit′ te′
Toa-ba
Hotok′ hotok′ te′
Atal-ba

Toa Ba

["Toa ba" *dai*
Full of blossom, dai
"Atal ba"

Full of fragrance
"Toa ba"
Full of whiteness
"Atal ba"

Let us pluck it
"Toa ba"
Let us break it
"Atal ba"

Come, we'll pick
Blossom of flowers
Come, we'll stich
Garland of flowers

Around the hair knot
"Toa ba"
Around the neck
"Atal ba"]

In the Mundari folklores, flower is the most referred part of a plant. Charmed by its beauty, it is often described in the songs. Forest flowers are used by the indigenous people to ornate themselves. For the religious rituals and festivals also, primarily flowers of the forest species are used and never the cultivated ones.

In this poetry "*Toa ba*" and "*Atal ba*" are mentioned as these are the two flowers that are one of the most referred species in the Munda songs.

"*Toa ba*" (*Holarrahea antidysenterica* Wall) is a forest species. As the Mundari name suggests the flowers are white as milk, "*Toa*" means milk and "*ba*" means flower. It has a very sweet fragrance. In the poem, a younger brother or sister is asking the elder sister "dai" to have a look at the beauty of the flower which is beautiful as well as fragrant. It is desired that both of them should pluck and pick the flower to tie it around the hair knot as it will enhance the beauty of the hair.

"*Atal ba*" (*Tabernaemontana divaricata* L. v. n. E: Crape Jasmine; H: Chandni) is yet another favourite. Enchanted by its beauty, it is suggested that both of them should collect the full bloomed white flowers of "*Atal ba*". It will then be stitched to put around the neck as garland which will enhance the beauty of the wearer.

The poetry here describes the beauty of two indigenous species along with its utility in native life. The song also depicts the uniqueness that is ascribed to flowers, the attribution of a singularity with which they maintain individualised relations.

2.
Guńgu

Ahré guńgu, bahre' gun'gu
Sakaam sańgom tem baiakana

Cetan redom jań gea,
Bitar redom jilu gea
Jargi jaram-jaram redo
Kami udam kuriko do

Amge hambud jat' koa
Amge gun'gud jat' kot

Gonoń tamak' huṛin' gea
Gun do tamak' purak gea

[*O Gun'gu*! O *Guńgu*!
You are made from leaves;
Outwardly you are stiff like bone,
But inner self is soft like flesh,
During the heavy rain,
The girl's work
In your embrace, you protect them,
Your price is less
But value is priceless.]

In a poetic sense, the poet has enumerated the qualities of *Gun'gu*. Tribal women are equal partakers in agriculture work. During the rainy season the females go to the paddy fields to do the paddy cropping. It is a tough task as the rain pours heavily at the time of season. To protect themselves, they wear a particular raincoat called "*Guńgu*" (*Bauhinia vahlli* wt & Arn. v. n. H: Mahulan, M: Gungu nari) which is a climber found in the forests. From the leaves of this particular plant, the many layered hood is stitched. It covers the back and the body and comes up to knee length. The front is open, thus with free hands they bend and do their work in the muddy fields. The hood is stiff like bone from outside but inward it is soft like flesh and gives warmth. Therefore, the poet denotes that in the embrace of "*Guńgu*", the working girls find shelter and protection from heavy rain. As made from leaves, it is available free of cost or a very little money is taken for stiching it. Usually, it is not sold. Its price may be less but evaluating its value it seems priceless.

The poem is a beautiful example of the affective status of useful objects in the life of the tribal woman. The '*gun'gu*' extends itself into a human dimension; it becomes an intimate audience and subject of love for the women agriculturist.

3.

Sahan agun seno redo
Sakạm hejem birid redo
O hore maina, Hora rem naki supi dena
Seta rem birida, roka tokam senoa
O hore maina, hora rem naki supi dena

Naki taben me gatim, supid taben me
Songe kodo ko nir bage langa

[If you go to collect firewood
If you go to pluck leaves
My dear, you comb your hair on the way

You got up early and proceeded hurriedly
My dear, you comb your hair on the way

Comb your hair and dress yourself quickly
We will be left behind by our colleagues.]

The actual village life and the share of work by the females are described in this song. It is the duty of the women to collect firewoods, leaves, and other forest produces. They are also well aware of their responsibility and accomplish it with sincerity.

In this song, the girls are proceeding to the forest for the collection of firewoods and leaves. Two friends are hurriedly preparing themselves to go to the forest. One is saying to the other that they have to go to the forest to collect firewood and leaves. Though her friend had got up early and had hurried, but she had no time to comb her hair. Her friend is telling her that they had to proceed and on the way she can comb her hair.

In the third stanza, one is telling the other to comb her hair and dress herself quickly, otherwise they will be left behind by their other friends who have already proceeded to the forest. In these lines, the tribal taboos are again focused, according to which the girls do not go to the forest alone but in group, and they are also wise enough and so they prefer to go in group. (Chapter 1, Tribal Taboos).

The way the toil of everyday life intersects with the instinct of beauty and joy in a tribal girl's life is evident in the song.

4.

Dolabu dai bir teho
Sahaֿn Sakaֿm agute
Sahaֿn Sakaֿm okoe agua bua
Apan jiu re bichare yabu bole

Sekerabu senoa
Tikin singi jeta-a
Jete lolo okoe sahatinga
Apaֿn jiu re bichare yabu bole

[Let us proceed to the forest, sister dear
To bring firewood and leaves
Otherwise, who will bring firewood and leaves for us
Let us think over it by ourselves for a moment

We shall proceed hurriedly
By noon it will become hot
Who will bear the scorching sun
Let us think over it by ourselves for a moment]

The song here focuses on two points, one is the requirement and the other is its honest fulfilment. It is the duty of the females to bring firewoods and leaves from the forest. Actually they collect firewood in the summer season, enough to store for the rainy season. In the rainy season, they won't get dry firewoods; therefore, they gather enough firewood in the hot summer month. It is a difficult task but they accomplish it with zeal.

To avoid the scorching sun they go to the forest early in the morning. (Ch. 1)

In the song, the younger sister is telling her elder sister that they should proceed to the forest to bring firewood and leaves. "If we will not go just think who else will do the work for us." It is their duty and no one else will perform it for them.

To avoid the heat of summer month, she is telling that they should proceed early in the morning, otherwise in the noon it will become very hot and it will be difficult to bear the scorching sun. "If we will not do accordingly just think who else will do the work which is of course, ours, for us." The lines show the intelligence and far-sightedness of the younger sister.

This song celebrates sisterhood and its associate emotions. Women's solidarity, their empathy for each other and the bond is expressed in the song. These are the inevitable gifts of being close to nature and to each other.

5.

Huṛing-huṛing gutu ṛe
Towa baha do baha len
Ho, hore, mai re
Ne bahaete oko baha re pura: sugaṛam

Huṛing-huṛing gutu re
Towa baha do baha len
Ho, hore, mai re
Towa bahaete Buṛju baha re pura-a: sugaṛam

[On a small hillock
Towa flower had bloomed
O daughter, dear

Leave aside this flower, on which flower
You will be more beautiful

On a small hillock
Towa flower had bloomed
O daughter, dear

You are more beautiful in *Buṛju* flower
than *Towa* flower]

Some crucial points have been emphasized in this poem. One is the affection and concern of a mother towards her daughter and the other is the tradition of the girls to decor themselves with the different flowers of the forest.

A mother is telling her daughter that on a small hillock "*Towa*" flower has bloomed (*Holarrehena antidysenetrica* Wall. *v.n.* H: Kurchi) which is a forest species much appreciated for its white scented flowers. It is a favourite flower of the girls as they use it to decor themselves. Mother is saying that the daughter should wear "*Towa*" baha to decorate herself. But soon she gives a second thought saying "*Buṛju*" flower will suit her more and she should wear "*Buṛju*" flower instead of "*Towa*" flower. "*Buṛju*" (*Bauhinia variegate* L. v. n. H: Kachnar) is found in the villages as well as forest. The leaves and flowers are edible. The purple colour flowers are also very beautiful.

Composed in the context of a mother's tender love for her daughter, this song enlivens the entire aesthetics of beauty and sensuous self-expression. The choice of the flowers, according to her mother is her meticulous exercise of love and expression of her desire to see her daughter in the most beautiful look. In an oblique way, it also allows the mother to live her own moments of romance through her daughter. It is evident that these values enjoy a glorious respect in the community.

6.

Chikan ará : gom side kena
Tereṇg kata go losodạn gi
Chikạn daṛi gom do: au kena

Suba Sunupid ba chuṭ reyaṛạn gi

Muchri ará : gom side kena
Tereṇg kata go losodận gi
Buchi daṛi gom da : au kena
Suba sunupid ba chuṭ reyaṛạn gi

[What vegetable did you pluck, O girl
Your legs are spoiled with mud
From which brook did you collect water, O girl
The roots of the hair-knot and tip of flowers yours are wet

You plucked *muchri* ará, O girl
Legs yours are spoiled with mud
You collected water from broken brook, dear
The roots of the hair-knot and tip of flower yours are wet]

The song here describes the conversation between two girls. The usual work of girls and habit and habitat of vegetation is also described.

The girl is enquiring about the *ará* (pot herb) she is collecting. She says that she must have gone to pick '*muchri ará* as her legs are soiled with mud.

"*Muchri*" (*Limnophila conferta* Benth) is a tender pot herb which grows on marshy land and shallow pools of water. Though it has a bitter taste, but it is eaten as a pot herb. It has great medicinal value. While collecting the plant, only few inches from the top is broken; the whole plant is not uprooted. Only a female has the patience and delicacy to pluck it; while gathering the pot herb it is sure to spoil ones feet due to the mud or wet soil.

The girl must have gone to fetch water from the broken brook, thus her hairknot and the flower pined in it is also wet.

The strong evocation of the rigour of the girls' life and the spirited engagement with it resonate in this song. It seems to represent the wonderful acceptance of life in all its colours of labour and love which is the hallmark of tribal life.

Kurukh Folklores

Khilbiri

Huram tockhe bahin komaḍxa inna
Koenchha nindiya, ambot deragon
ẋedo pojjra hiya gamchha banna
Barach isan ēray khilibiri re

Guchaya hiya akku edapa kirrot
Mandi khat-ot, tanik komaḍxa dim
Amadi gane tanik kanjji irtot
Panhe nēka ẋollot ẋolṭot nehuñ edapa nu malikaya re

[Today pluck all "*komaḍxa*" my sister
Our "*Koenchha*" is full, come let us go home,
Sister in law, come here, see the "*khilibiri*" flower
Come friend, now let us go home
We will cook rice and *"komaḍxa"* also
will add a little in the rice starch water.]

In this poem, the poet has presented a real picture of tribal women's life. The poem puts forth the women who went to the forest for collecting various articles of their use. One woman is saying to another that they had plucked enough "*komaḍxa" Bauhinia purpurea* L.V.n. Koenar and pointed that they should not to ignore the "*khilibiri"* flower. They had put all these articles in their "*Koenchha"* and finishing their work for that day, they can now proceed for their home. At home, they cook rice and in the starchy soup of rice they add a little "*komaḍxa"* which they had brought from the forest.

The biodiversity of the region has been noted with various forest species like beautiful rose pink "*khilibiri"* (*Indigo pulchella* Roxb. v. n. M, S: Hutar, N: Jirhul, K: Khilibiri), "*deragon*" (*Antidesma diandrum* Roxb. v.n. H: Amta sag; M: Mata ará; S: Matha arak; Ku: deragon). All the above mentioned species are edible and are popular as pot herbs.

The poetry explains the beautiful custom which prevails among tribal women. All of them— sister, sister in law, Sahiya etc.—may not have blood relations, but they address each other cordially as they work in unison. Sahiya is a special friendship bond a woman prevails with another woman who is very dear to her. They call each other with name usually of a flower.

It describes the dressing sense of women and its utility. "*Koincha*" is a part of the *Sari* they wear, which is tied in front and is used to put the collected light weight articles like plucked flowers, leaves, pot herbs etc.

The simple lifestyle of the village is also focused. Though the women had returned from the forest, they do not relax after their hard work. Their cooking is very simple. Usually they cook rice and in the starchy soup they put the pot herbs and leaves which they have collected. It is known as "*Manr jhor*". Tribal life is well explained in the poetry.

Konch

Pairi pairi kalahi madagi mannan
Mēn ēra chandi pum̄p kōnchad ho
Judi pello gahi bindo khopa bese
Sonarakhi lavapan ti lav-karaki be-e̱ ei ho

Bidi potthare- e madagi khatri – e
Addo oye bar-ee, monx̣a ho
Pellar barnar kummar baugi khaichlan
Aar sangge ning judi pello mal ietha ri-ee họ

[Early in the morning go near the "*mahua*" tree
Look, the flower buds shining like silver,
Scattered in the ground,
Shining as "sonarakhi"
in a young girl's hair.

Sun rises, the "*mahua*" flowers drops
Cows and cattles graze it
The girl's come with *kumver. bogi, khaichla* to collect the flowers]

The song composer is enchanted by the beauty of the flower. This song depicts the physiological process of dropping of "*mahua*" (*Madhuca indica* Gmel. v. n. H: Mahua). The process of dropping of *mahua* flowers is very precise; it does not drop simultaneously but only one by one. Furthermore, the dropping time is also fixed; it drops in the wee hours of morning.

The poet is amazed by the beauty of the dropped flower which glitters like silver buds scattered beneath the tree. It is as beautiful and shining as "*Sonarakhi*" (*Cassia fistula.* v. n. H: Amaltas) flower that is suitable for enhancing beauty of a girl by tucking it in her hairs. It is also useful for the cattles, as they come beneath the tree to graze it. The indigenous tradition is also explained early in the morning, *mahua* flowers are collected only by the girls and children. They carry with them *"Kumver", "bogi"* and *"Khachila"* which are the traditional baskets of different size and are made of bamboos. These baskets are used to collect things. Indigenous life pattern and the labour of women are well explained in the song.

One cannot fail to notice the intimate relation with nature that is developed through these songs. Nature, in these songs, is not merely a collection of beautiful objects to be enjoyed but is a field of emotions in which the natural objects merge seamlessly with the senses of the women.

Lau Jhunda

Lau punūpan mejhra-ay hiya
Parta Karga hiyo re pàaḍ-di
Paahi khēta soḍage ba-ar neen
Atakḥa sabaḍ sabaḍ chokdi

Parhe parta lau jhuñd hiya
utaḳhi ataḳha amake kudda
Khañḍon lao laḍang nu jhota ēr–ar
utaḳhi amke se natga bedda

Bhare asaaḍ, nu podho dabolta
Lao jhuñd num dokh lakra re
Langaḍi pachhon dharcha mo-kha
Lau jhuñd aungem e-ra e-ra korke re

Inna aal khonḍh ad hūn– ennem hiya
Eksan lakadad eksan merahod
Thaach thahach ek ke hiya

Dhokha kahiyo amake mocha re.

[Adorning the hair with red flowers
You sing while climbing the hill
to give food in the *"dona-sora"* to the guests
You pluck the leaves quickly

In the nearby hill, there are plenty of bushes
Don't roam about alone
Watch while cutting the bushes
Don't ever try to pull it alone.

In the rainy season
Two hyena were there
They have caught and eaten
The lame old woman
Watch while you enter the bushes

Today human are just like hyena
No difference between animal and man
Carefully you lead life
Don't ever be deceived

In this song, the geography and biodiversity of the land is well explained. A girl is climbing up the hill while singing, and has adorned her hair with red flowers. She is quickly plucking leaves with which she will make "*dona sora*" in which she will serve food to the guests. She is in a hurry. It may be that the guests have already arrived at home.

The daily life of a tribal girl is well explained here. The girls and women have the task to pluck the leaves from the forest and make "*dona sora*", that is, leaf plates and cups in which food is served to the guests.

The poet warns the girl about the dangers of the forest. He advises her that she should not roam about in the forest alone. She should be watchful while cutting the bushes and never pull it alone. He warns about the wildlife of the woods. In the rainy season, two hyenas were behind the bushes and had caught and eaten a lame old woman who was cutting the bushes. The work performed by both young and old woman is explained along with the possibility of her becoming victim of the dangers of the forest.

The poetry takes a philosophical turn. The song writer says that today there is no difference between men and wild animals, as both destroy women's life. He advises the young girl that she should lead her life carefully and never be caught and never be deceived. The entire narrative reeks of a careful observation of the precarious existence of the women, and situates their lives amid physical and psychological dangers. In a sense, this is a song of the collective fears lodged in the hearts of the tribal women.

Rim rimira-aa birhaa laaggi
Madgi khatera-aa laaggi
Khatera-aa chiaa bhaiya khatera-aa chiaa ho
Peloge pesage bhaar-mana laaggi

[Soft sunlight is spreading out
Mahua is dropping
Let it fall brother, let it fall
The young woman will have no difficulty
In picking them up.]

This poem is an amalgamation of beauty of nature and human life. The process of dropping of "*Madgi*" (*Madhuca indica* Gmel. v.n. H: Mahua) is unique. It drops one by one from the tree since the wee hours of morning. Slowly the sun rises and the soft morning rays spread out. It is enchanting to see the beautiful flowers in the soft morning light. It seems that the slowly spreading sunlight is caressing the Mahua flowers.

Moreover, the poem again puts forth the culture and duty of women. It is the women's task to collect the "*Mahua*" flowers. The poet is telling the boy that the flowers should fall and the young women will pick it up without difficulty.

Kirha Kirha ba-adi pelo
Haye kirha ainw ula raao ho
Tundsin dharoye pelo
Komaarhkhan tokwoye
haye kirha ainw ula raao ho

[Hunger! Hunger! you mutter O maid!

Oh! How long will hunger last?
Will you hold the tongs, O dame?
Will you pluck spinach of Koenar?
Oh! How long will hunger last?]

This poem explains the struggle for survival of life. The poet feels pity for a woman who is in a faminished state. He says that you are muttering hunger but the survival is in your own hand. She should hold the clutch and pluck the "*komaḍxa*" leaves. With this she can satisfy her hunger.

The agriculture pattern of the region is such that the rice grains are sufficient only for six months. In the summer months, rice grains are not available sufficiently so they take the aid of edible forest's flowers, fruits, various leaves and pot herbs to satisfy their hunger. To pluck the leaves or flowers that grow on the top part of trees they make a sort of clutch with long stick and with its help they pluck the leaves and flower and break the fruits. The women collect these articles and satisfy their own hunger as well as fulfil the need of the family.

++"*komaḍxa*" (*Bauhinia purpurea* L. v. n. H: Koenar) is one of such tree species. The new leaves sprout in the months of May and are popular because it is edible. Its utility is such that it is often described in the folklores.

Kharia Folklores

1.

Gungu te jatane boi joi
lo: dho: barkha no dena
kuwar batik te barkha dena
gungu te jatane boi joi

[Keep the Gungu with care O! *Boi Joi*
it will rain again
In *kuwar, Kartik*
it will rain again
keep the *Gungu* with care O! *Boi joi*]

Women are the partakers in the cropping system. Often they take the aid of forest species to accomplish their work. This truth is explained beautifully in this poem. The composer of the song is asking his sister and daughter to keep the "*Gungu*" with care because after the rainy season it will drizzle occassionly again in *Kuwar* (October) and Kartik (November) during which "*Gungu*" will be used again. Therefore, they should keep the "*Gungu*" carefully.

"*Gungu*" is a kind of hood made of *Bauhinia vahlli* wt & Arn. V.n. H: Mahulan; M: Gungu nari, leaves. It is stitched in such a way that it covers the head and body little below the knees, whereas the front is open and the women have no difficulty in sowing the paddy crops in the rainy season. Not only in the rainy season but it is useful in other months also. This traditional hood is made of leaves of the forest species which comes for free but its stiching is difficult and takes much time. Its value as an aid in doing the agriculture work is great. Therefore, it is kept carefully at home. "*Gungu*" is another forest species which is described often in the folklores.

2.

Anna-anna boi pudu: b ramna
Theitka dho: ke hotraiga chonam
Anna-anna boi pudu: b ramna

[Let us go, boi, to pick *pudu*
Hold the *Theitka*
Pick while walking
Let us go, boi, to pick *pudu*]

In this song, sheer joy and excitement of gathering the seasonal forest produces is described. A girl is asking her *boi* (sister) to go with her to collect "*pudu*" (*lycoperdon bovista.* v. n. E: Puff ball; M, S: Putka; N: Rugra). It grows in the soil during the rainy season as small white balls and its availability is only for a short time. It is considered very tasty and a great delicacy. People in the village look forward in picking up this "*pudu*". Usually, while picking these up, women and children take a small basket and chisel (*khurpi*) and keep digging the soil slightly. Though a tedious task, it is a happy time which everyone enjoys.

3.

Sinkom joiri nana joi
Seirga ra:ra:shi
Ana nana chonanang
Soriga baejana
Ana nana chonanang
Soriga baejana
Diri rirei gamo: vere
kocha te sire njoigenang
njo:na udna ejo umbo nana
kocha te sire njoigenang

[Like stars oh! *"nana joi"*
"Seirga" has blossomed
Come *"nana"*, both will go
to collect *"Seirga"*
When clouds will thunder
We will boil it in the corner and eat
When nothing to eat, oh! "*nana*"
We will boil it in the corner and eat.]

The natural tendency and wisdom of the females to preserve the food articles when it is available and use it later at the time of adversity is described in this song. The dependency on the forest species to combat hunger is also made clear. In this Kharia song, a girl is telling her "*nana joi*" i.e. elder sister about "*Seirga*" (fruit of *Shorea robusta* Gaertn. v. n. H: Sal) has blossomed like stars in the forest. It is high time for them to go and collect it. In the rainy season when there is nothing to eat at home, they will boil it in the cornor and eat. They boil it in the corner because it is not the main food; hence kitchen is not used for it.

The most remarkable aspect of these songs is their dialogic character. They are in the form of dialogues that constitute the conversations between the women, representing all episodes of their lives. The range of the tone varies from personal anxieties to collective joys.

4.

Koleng pinjna cholkim no boi
Jhimir Jhimir da: no delta
Jono:h japud cholkim noo boi
Jhimir jhimir Da: no delta

[O! Daughter has gone to collect *"Karil"*
And it is raining
O! Daughter has gone to collect *"Jono"*
And it is raining]

The folklore shows the concern of parents for their daughter. They are anxious that it has started raining and their daughter has gone out to collect "*Karil*". They are afraid that she may be dreanched in the rain. "*Karil*" is the new shoots of bamboo *bambusa* sp. V. n. H: *Bans*, which comes out during the rainy season. It is edible and people relish it. Pickle (Sandhana – Ch. 3) is also made of it. It is used at home as well as sold in the market. They are worried that their daughter has gone out to collect "*Jono*" and it is raining. "*Jono*" is a grass of *Andropogen muricatus* Retz. v.n. H: Khas; S: Sirom; M: Jono' tasad, and is used to make broom. It is used at home as well as sold.

The poet denotes the responsibility of the daughter or the women- folk of the house to bring the household articles which may also be a means of sustenance.

5.

Koienjy'ra Rori biru te
Songol ga no pije
Ulla: ga no pije
Anargi no pije
Gamo;b no re nana joi
Umbra: maha: Biru te
Songol ga no pije
Ulla:h ga noo pije
Anargi noo pije
Gamo:b noo re nana joi

Pailkota Sahar te
Le Bari kathi, Le Bari patoi
Le Bara datun
Gamkon si jeoin re nana joi

[On the Roli hills of *Koienjy'ra*
Collect the woods!
Pluck the leaves!
Break the toothbrush stick!
You always said, *O! Nana joi,*
On the big hill of *Umra*
Collect the woods!
Pluck the leaves!
Break the tooth brush sticks!
You always said, O! *Nana joi*
In the city of Palkot
Take, aunty! woods, take, aunty! leaves
take, Uncle! tooth brush sticky's
You always called while
You did *"Kheza"*]

This Kharia song depicts a fondness though it even puts forth the sad remembrance of a girl about her *nana joi* (elder sister). She may be small when she used to go with her elder sister to the hills and forests. Here the description of going to Roli hills of *Koienjy'ra* and big hill of *Umra* is made. In the forest, the elder one used to ask her little sister to collect woods, leaves, and tender shoot which would be used as toothbrush. Actually the elder sister is teaching her ways of recognizing and the art of collecting the useful items. Together they will take all the gathered forest goods to the city of Palkot (a place near Ranchi). The little girl watched her elder sister crying out to the customers so that they buy her collected articles. Very cordially she will call them as *Bari*, aunty and *Bara* uncle and request them to buy *Kathi* i.e fire woods, *Patoi* i.e. leaves, *Dhatun*, i.e. toothbrush sticks etc. The elder sister will do "*Kheza*" of the saleable item. In the villages, the people often sell their forest produces not by weighing but put them in small heaps and take little amount of money for each heap.

The song reflects the struggling life of a girl and her younger sister. It shows the stark importance of forest for the livelihood of villagers. The last two lines of the song are in "Sadri" or "Nagpuria" which shows the change of vocabulary from village to town accordingly.

Ho Folklores

'Ho' Durang

1.

Sarajom dishum mere dada
Nalo rem gohingha dada
Madhukam dishum mere dada
Nalorem chalingha dada!!

Sarajom dishum doya dada
Singi laya-laya dada
Madhukam dishum doya dada
Nida rawana, rubung dada!!

[Do not marry me, O Dada
In a village where its *"Sarjom"* tree
Do not marry me, O Dada

In a village where its *"Madhukam"* tree
In a village where its *"Sarjom"* tree
Whole day, under the sun
I'll be picking *"Sarjom"*

In a village where its *"Madhukam"* tree
Since mid night, beneath the tree
I'll be picking *"Madhukam"*
Bending and picking
My back will ache.

In this song, a girl of marriageable age is requesting her *dada* (elder brother) not to give her in marriage to a village where there are "*Sarjom*" and "*Madhukam*" trees. She says that in a village where there are "*Sarjom*" trees, she will have to spend whole day under the sun picking and collecting "*Sarjom*". Furthermore, if she will be sent by marriage to a village where there are "*Madhukam*" trees, then since mid night she will have to go and pick "*Madhukam*" under the tree. Every time she will have to bend to pick her back will ache.

"*Sarjom*" (*Shoera robusta* Gaertn. v.n. H: Sal) and "*Madhukam*"

(*Madhuca indica* Gmel. v.n. H: Mahua) are the two forest species which can be considered as pillars of sustainence to a tribal life. The Sal fruits drop during the hot summer months. The fruits are collected for its multifarious utility. These are edible and can be called famine food (Ch. 3) that are used as medicine as well as sold in the market to fetch money etc. Due to its many utilities, it is gathered in the season. Mahua is yet another species of economic importance. The Mahua flowers are eaten and can be called famine food (Chapter 3). The flowers are sold fresh and fetches good money as country liquor is made from it. It has medicinal properties also. The flowers do not drop simultaneously but one by one during the wee hours of the morning, and it is a tedious task to collect the dropping flowers.

Usually, it is the task of women to collect the Sal fruits and Mahua flowers. Due to its great utility, it is mandatory for them to gather it. These fruits and flowers are of course seasonal and to gather the Sal fruits one has to stand under the tree to gather them in the hot summer season. To collect Mahua flowers, one has to start gathering it from mid night or very early morning. These trees are large and hence one cannot climb on it. It is also customary to wait for its dropping. Every time one has to bend to pick it up; it may cause back ache.

The social right is also reflected. The forest trees are the property of the whole society; no one can claim for the forest species. Whoever comes early gathers the fruits and flowers. It is a simple law and is never disputed.

The social ritual is also signified. The elder brother holds a key position in the family regarding the marriage of his younger sister. The parents always consult him and sought his opinion. His affection is also there for his sister. Therefore, the girl finds it easy to approach him and she is sure of his affection and also his position at home as his advice will be counted by their parents.

2.

Bar a dope bar a guri tana mai!!
dali dope, duli noder tana
thore-thope tan naka kanam mai!!
Hirka tapa kam tiki kena!!
thore-thope kam naka mai!!
Bonga mandi koko nema leya.

[Today, are you celebrating *"ba"* *O mai*!
You are using cowdung for the festival
You are keeping *Sarjom* branches
inside the courtyard, *O mai*!
You are adorning your hair with flowers
Look, half of the flowers are dropping out
You are putting so much of flowers
in your hair knot]

The song writer is looking at the preparations of Baha festival from the perspective of a girl. "*Mai*" is a Ho word by which the girls are commonly addressed. "*Baha*" festival is the festival of flowers celebrated during spring season. Usually like any other festival, the responsibility of arrangements generally comes in the female's hand. As the girl is busy, the poet is asking her if today she is celebrating "*Baha*" festival. He observes that she has cleaned her courtyard with cowdung, and in the clean place she is keeping the branches of "*Sarjom*". She is also preparing herself for the festival. In ecstasy, she has put on so many flowers in her hair that half of the flowers are falling out.

The atmosphere of festival celebration is well described. It is the responsibility of the lady of the house and daughter to make the house ready for the day. It is the ritual that she has to clean the house and courtyard with cowdung. It is supposed to purify the soil and atmosphere. The flowering branches of "*Sarjom*" (*Shorea robusta* Gaertn. v. n. H: Sal) which has been brought from the forest by the males of the house is kept inside properly. Sal is worshipped during the festival of "*Baha*". Nevertheless, she does not ignore herself but makes herself beautiful by adorning her hair with flowers.

Like many other beautiful songs, this song also portrays how the entire atmosphere of festivities pervades the individual spirit and yet the balance between the personal and social spheres is not disturbed.

3.

Okon koreya badan tana
lova ba nagra do sohwan tana
Okon kore ko dulin tana
niche ba rodo songa choroyor kena

Negam kudi chaka bara tana
lova ba nagra do Sohan tana
dungura kuri ba chako dali tana
niche ba rodo singa chod royar kena

[Where "*ba*" is being celebrated?
Seems sound of drum beating
From "*lova*" flower is coming
Where branch of flower is kept?

Fragrance of "*Icha*" flower is coming
In the neighbouring village "*ba*" is being celebrated
Thus drum beating is echoing
In the neighbouring village
Women are adorning hair with flowers
Thus fragrance of flower is coming

A person is puzzled and is questioning about the whereabout of the "*ba*" festival. For him it seems as if the sound of "*nagra*", that is, the drum beating is coming from "*lova*" flowers. He also smells the fragrance of "*Icha*" flower and is amazed if it is kept somewhere near. He gets the answer that "*ba*" festival is being celebrated in the neighbouring village and from there only, the sound of celebrations is coming. The women of the neighbouring village are adorning their hair with "*Icha*" flowers for the festival and therefore the fragrance of flower is coming.

"*Ba*" or "*Baha Parob*" is the festival of flowers. During spring time Sal, Palas and many more forest species bloom. The forest becomes colourful and fragnant by the flowers. The word meaning of "*Ba*" or "*Baha*" is flower. Tribals are nature worshippers, and they worship the trees and flowers at this spring time. It is also a time to rejoice. The festive mood is well described here. The tribes beat their "*nagara*" that is a particular drum with great echoing sound. The sound travels to the nearby villages, hills and forests. The joyous mood can well be calculated from far away. Here the person is not questioning directly but takes the aid of a poetic sense, of "*lova*" (*Ficus glomerata* Roxb. v. n. H: Gular). The flower of Gular cannot be seen due to its peculiar inflorescence. During the festivals, the women do not adorn themselves with any cultivated flowers but they décor their hairs with the forest species only. "*Icha*" *(Woodfordia fruticosa* L. v. n. H: Dawai), is one of such species. It has beautiful orange colour and has a sweet fragrance. The village life of tribes is well explained.

4.

Nora re sarjom ba
Tiheyo ko tebaoh

Natu re hende hapanum
Mocha teya kay kappa jiya

Chaku to laipe, titeyo kateybao
Sutam kulaipe mocha teyo kay ka paji

Chaku tolaipe bankiya rapud jana
dutam kul lena
dutamo katay rapud jana

[Sarjom flowers in the path
cannot be reached by hand
dusky damsel of the village
do not answer when called
"*bankiya*" is made to pluck the flowers

But it broke before plucking
"dutam" is send for her
but oh! he also broke his leg]

The composer of the lines above reveals the feeling of a young boy. The boy is symbolising a girl whom he loves with "*Sarjom*" (*Shorea robusta* Gaertn. v. n. H: Sal) flowers. He says she is beautiful but unaprochable like Sal flowers in the path which is in such height that it is out of reach. Clutch is made to reach and pluck the flowers but alas, it also broke. Thus the flowers were not plucked. The beautiful dusky girl of the village is also somewhat difficult to reach. She never answers when he tries to speak to her. A messenger was sent to approach her, but unfortunately he also broke his leg and thus his mission was not fulfilled.

In the tribal poetry, it is comman to symbolize a young girl or boy with forest flowers or birds etc. Here the poet has put forth the simple process of breaking flower and fruit which grow at a good height. For this act, help of "*bankiya*" is taken. "*Bankiya*" is a kind of clutch. It is a long stick before its extreme end another small stick is fastened vertically. This portion is twisted to break the flowers and fruits.

The social custom of marriage is also explained. In the tribes, the parents of a boy or girl never negotiate the marriage personally. Help of another person "*dutam*", messenger or go between is taken. The message is always send from the boy's side and not *vice versa*. After much thinking, the messagner is given a positive or negative answer. Thus, the feeling of the other side is not hurt directly.

Bibliography

Aditya, Alok. *Song of the Woods*, Jagriti Vihara, Centre of Education for Rural Reconstruction, Mc Cluskieganj, India.

"Adivasi", (2007), Murmu, Babulal. Soros Sereng. Santhali Sahitya Prasarak Seva Mandal, Dumka, Jharkhand.

Archer, W.G., (1940), *The Blue Groove: The Poetry of the Oraons*. London: George Allan Unicoin.

Archer, W.G., H. Durang

Archer, W.G., *The Hills of Flutes*. Isha Books, Delhi.

Bhattacherjee, S.K., (2004), *Handbook of Medicinal Plants*. Pointer Publishers, Jaipur.

Bodding, P.O. (1916), *Some Remarks on the Position of Women among the Santhals*. Journal of the Bihar and Orissa Research Society.

Bodding, P.O., (1926), *Studies in Santhal Medicine and Connected Folklore*, The Asiatic Society, Kolkata.

Bodding, P.O., (2002), *A Santhal Dictionary*, Gyan Publishing House, New Delhi. 2002.

Demta, Sukhram, Munda Chamra, *Mundari Puthi, Class 2*, Mundari Bhasa Text Book Committee, Ranchi, Jharkhand.

Ganguli, Satya, K. (1958), *A Few Munda and Oraon Folksongs*, Indian Folklore, Vol. 1.

Hains, H.H. (1961), *The Botany of Bihar and Orissa*. Government of Bihar and Orissa.

Hembrom, P.P. (1994), *Adivasi Aushad*, Paharia Sewa Samiti, Satia, Pakur.

Hoffmann, J., Emelen, A.V. (2009), *Encyclopaedia Mundarica*, Gyan Publishing House, New Delhi.

Jain, S.K. (1991), *A Manual of Ethno Botany*, Scientific Publishers, Jodhpur.

Jain, S.K., (1968), *Medical Plants*, National Book Trust, India.

Joshi, P.C., Joshi, Namita. *A Textbook of Ecology and Environment*. Himalaya Publishing House.

Kandya, A.K., Gupta, Asha (2007). *Biodiversity Conservation and Legal Aspects.* Aavishkar Publisher, Jaipur.

Munda, Kande (2008), *Sasan Ba Peele Phool*, Bhaiya Ram Munda Foundation, Ranchi, Jharkhand.

Mundu, M.M. (1995), *Mundari Dictionary*. L.W.F/DMD Asia Desk, Geneva.

Pandey, Deep Narain. Singh, Samar (1996), *Beyond Vanishing Woods*, Himanshu Publications, Udaipur.

Patnaik, Nityanand (2002), *Folklore of Tribal Communities*. Gyan Publishing House, New Delhi.

Prasad, Dineshwar, (1979), *Hoffma on Mundari Poetry*, Jyoti Publication, Patna.

Singh, J.P.; Vyas, N.N. and Mann, R.S. (1988), *Tribal Women and Development.* Rawat Publications, Jaipur.

Singh, V., Jain, D.K. (2002), *Taxonomy of Angiosperms*, Rastogi Publications, Meerut.

Sinku, Daymanti. *Ho Janjati Me Ba Geet: Ek Adhyayan.*

Tirkey, M.L. (2009), *Shilagayn*. Publisher, L. Tirkey. New Delhi.

Topno, Sem., (2004), *Musical Culture of the Munda Tribe*. Concept Publishing Company, New Delhi.

Toppo (Kullu), Ignasiya, (2004), *Kharia Lok Geeton Ki Pechan*. Publisher Dr. Ignasia toppo (Kullu).

Trivedi, P.C. (2002), *Ethnobotany*, Aavishkar Publishers, Jaipur.

Trivedi, P.C. (2009), *Medical Plant Utilisation and Conservation*, Aavishkar Publishers.

Troup, R.S. (2007), *Manual of Indian Forest Utilization*. Asiatic Publishing House, New Delhi.

Verma, S.K. (1998), Srivastava, D., Pandey, A.K., *Ethnobotany of Santhal Parganas*, Narendra Publishing House. New Delhi.

Index